Brain
Food

hamlyn

Brain Food

the essential guide
to boosting your
brain power

Lorraine Perretta
recipes by Oona van den Berg

A Pyramid Paperback from Hamlyn

First published in Great Britain in 2001 by
Hamlyn, a division of Octopus Publishing Group Ltd
2–4 Heron Quays, London E14 4JP

This edition first published in 2004
Copyright © Octopus Publishing Group Ltd 2001, 2004

ISBN 0 600 61088 8

A CIP catalogue record for this book is available from the
British Library

Printed and bound in China

10 9 8 7 6 5 4 3 2 1

All reasonable care has been taken in the preparation of this
book but the information it contains is not intended to take
the place of treatment by a qualified medical practitioner.

The Authors

Lorraine Perretta is a nutrition consultant with her own
practice in London. Lorraine graduated with honours from
LeMoyne College in New York and continued her education
in London at the Institute for Optimum Nutrition where she
has been a tutor and lecturer since 1996. Her written work
has been featured in a number of publications including
Vogue, *GQ* and *GQ Active*.

Oona van den Berg is a food writer and food stylist.
She has worked on a variety of magazines and was the food
editor on *Taste* and *Cosmopolitan* before spending two
years travelling through Asia in search of markets and
village life. She has also written recipes for *Miracle Foods*,
also published by Hamlyn.

Notes

Both metric and imperial measurements have been given in
all recipes. Use one set of measurements only, and not a
mixture of both.

Standard level spoon measurements are used in all recipes.

1 tablespoon = one 15 ml spoon

1 teaspoon = one 5 ml spoon

Eggs should be large unless otherwise stated. The
Department of Health advises that eggs should not be
consumed raw. This book contains dishes made with raw or
lightly cooked eggs. It is prudent for more vulnerable people
such as pregnant and nursing mothers, invalids, the elderly,
babies and young children to avoid uncooked or lightly
cooked dishes made with eggs. Once prepared, these
dishes should be kept refrigerated and used promptly.

Milk should be full fat unless otherwise stated.

This book includes dishes made with nuts and nut
derivatives. It is advisable for readers with known allergic
reactions to nuts and nut derivatives and those who may be
potentially vulnerable to these allergies, such as pregnant
and nursing mothers, invalids, the elderly, babies and
children to avoid dishes made with nuts and nut oils. It is
also prudent to check the labels of pre-prepared ingredients
for the possible inclusion of nut derivatives.

Pepper should be freshly ground black pepper unless
otherwise stated.

Fresh herbs should be used, unless otherwise stated. If
unavailable, use dried herbs as an alternative, but halve the
quantities stated.

Ovens should be pre-heated to the specified temperature –
if using a fan-assisted oven, follow the manufacturer's
instructions for adjusting the time and the temperature.

Vegetarians should look for the 'V' symbol on a cheese to
ensure it is made with vegetarian rennet. There are vegetarian
forms of Parmesan, feta, Cheddar, Cheshire, Red Leicester,
dolcelatte and many goats' cheeses, among others.

contents

the brain

The brain is the body's most complex organ. Not only is it the organ of thought, speech and emotion, it is also the main control centre of the body – controlling everything from basic functions such as heart rate and breathing to more complex areas such as sex drive, memory and mood. Throughout life the brain is constantly busy receiving sensations, processing and storing information, generating thoughts and emotions and storing memories. The nutrients in the food we eat are needed to keep the brain in top working order.

Neuronal structure

A nerve cell transmits messages throughout the brain

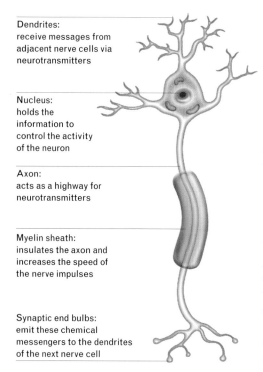

Dendrites:
receive messages from adjacent nerve cells via neurotransmitters

Nucleus:
holds the information to control the activity of the neuron

Axon:
acts as a highway for neurotransmitters

Myelin sheath:
insulates the axon and increases the speed of the nerve impulses

Synaptic end bulbs:
emit these chemical messengers to the dendrites of the next nerve cell

Although the adult human brain is small in comparison with the rest of the body, weighing only 1.5 kg (3 lb) and making up just 2 per cent of the body's total weight, it receives nearly one-fifth of the total oxygen and blood supply. This reflects the importance of the brain for good health and for life. When you think about the complex functions the brain can perform, it is not surprising that the body gives it such priority. For example, the brain of someone engaged in playing tennis can assess the speed and direction of an approaching ball, then organize the muscles in the legs and arms into hitting the ball, all while thinking about what to cook for dinner!

Vital nutrients carried in the blood are needed to enable the brain to perform such remarkable feats. These are filtered into the brain and converted, via complex reactions, into energy and the chemicals needed to make the system work. Without the correct balance of nutrients in the diet, the brain cannot give its peak performance.

Understanding the brain and its associated nervous system is an enormous challenge. The brain is the centre for receiving, processing and storing information. It makes decisions and directs action based on these decisions. It is also the centre of intellect, emotion and creativity. We are still at the very early stages of understanding how the brain carries out its many functions. In this chapter, we will look at how the human brain works and which nutrients are needed to optimize its function.

Neurons and messengers

The human brain has the consistency of very firm jelly and contains around 100 billion nerve cells called neurons. Each neuron has several branching tentacles and a thread-like filament called an axon, along which electrical impulses can pass. The neurons in the brain are usually only a few millimetres (less than half an inch) long, while the nerve cells in other parts of the body, for example

those that control movement in the toes, can reach almost 1 metre (3 feet) in length.

At the ends of the axons are many little bulbs, called synaptic end bulbs, which contain tiny amounts of chemicals called neurotransmitters. When the nerve cell is stimulated, these neuro-transmitters are released into the gap between one nerve cell and the next. This then stimulates the dendrites of the neighbouring cell. This neuron then releases its own neurotransmitters, stimulating the next cell to do likewise, and so on. In this way, millions of messages are passed from neuron to neuron every minute of the day.

There are about 60 known or suspected chemical neurotransmitters in the human nervous system and there are probably more to be discovered. Some of the more familiar ones are serotonin, endorphins, noradrenaline (also called norepinephrine) and acetylcholine. Although we are not sure what they all do, we do know that diet influences the type and activity of these chemicals and that they have powerful effects on our emotions.

Neurotransmitters are made from amino acids found in protein foods, such as meat, fish and cheese. Vitamins and minerals in the diet are key ingredients which we need to convert ordinary amino acids into these powerful neuromessengers. These nutrients will ensure that the brain completes functions with speed and efficiency.

Another important substance in the brain is fat, which is essential in both the structure and function of the brain. Surprisingly, the brain is more than 60 per cent fat. This is because every nerve cell in the brain is surrounded by a membrane composed of fat molecules. Many of these nerve cells are also insulated by a myelin sheath, which increases the speed of the nerve impulse conduction. The myelin sheath is composed of approximately 75 per cent fat. In addition to their important role in the brain's structure, fats play another crucial role as messengers, regulating aspects of immunity, circulation, inflammation, memory and mood.

Quick thinking

In some ways, the brain and nervous system act as the body's messenger service. The brain is the 'dispatch centre' while the nerve cells form an information network carrying messages all around the body.

Neurotransmitters are the 'messengers' carrying messages from neuron to neuron. These messengers can travel at great speeds, in some cases reaching a speed of around 450 kmph (280 mph)!

Feeding the brain

The brain has an extensive blood supply. There is a constant flow of blood carrying important neuro-nutrients, such as amino acids, vitamins and minerals, together with oxygen and glucose (a type of sugar) to provide energy for the brain. An interruption in the blood flow for just one or two minutes can impair brain function, resulting in confusion or unconsciousness; if the brain cells are deprived of oxygen for four minutes then permanent brain damage may occur. Good circulation and strong, healthy blood vessels are therefore vital for keeping the brain well fed.

The structure of the brain is so important that the body guards it with several shields against damage. There is not only the physical protection of the skull and underlying membranes but also a system called the blood-brain barrier, which protects against any poisons in the blood. The blood-brain barrier provides a filtration system, which allows only oxygen, glucose (sugar) and a few selected nutrients to pass through. Unfortunately, this barrier is not foolproof; although it allows essential nutrients and some mood-elevating substances to enter the brain, other chemicals including alcohol, nicotine and caffeine can also pass through to the brain with less beneficial effects.

Mental building blocks

A vast array of nutrients are needed to keep the brain working in top order. The neurons need to be fed in order to be able to carry strong, clear messages, the supporting structures need to be properly maintained so that the messengers have a smooth uninterrupted trip, and the whole of the nervous system needs lots of fuel to power vigorous mental activity. Good-quality food is essential as it provides the raw materials to build and fuel brain power.

The energy required to fuel the brain, and maintain healthy nerve cells and neurotransmitters, comes from the food we eat. And it is the nutrients in our food that provide the vital mental building blocks. The key nutrients to sustain and promote physical and mental activities are water, proteins, carbohydrates, fats, vitamins and minerals.

Key nutrients

Each of these nutrients has a vital role to play in building brain power and maintaining good physical and mental health.

Water

Water makes up 83 per cent of blood and acts as a transport system, delivering nutrients to the brain and carrying away waste products. A good supply of clean water is essential for concentration and alertness.

Proteins

Protein is found in meat, fish, milk, cheese, beans and grains. Components of protein provide the structural building materials for most of the body's tissues, nerves and internal organs, including the heart and brain. Proteins are also used to manufacture neurotransmitters as well as to build and maintain the nerve network. Proteins are essential for improving mental functions as well as lifting spirits.

Carbohydrates

Carbohydrates are found in grains, fruits and vegetables. Through digestion these carbohydrates break down into a sugar called glucose, which provides the brain with its primary source of energy. It is vital that this level of glucose does not fluctuate too much, otherwise mental confusion, dizziness, convulsions and loss of consciousness could occur.

Fats

There are three types of fat in food: saturated, monounsaturated and polyunsaturated fats. The term 'essential fatty acids' refers to two specific polyunsaturated fats called omega-6 and omega-3. Studies of essential fatty acids suggest that these special fats can increase brain size and brain cell numbers, improve vision and aid learning. Good sources of essential fatty acids are salmon, mackerel, sardines, nuts and seeds.

Vitamins and minerals

Vitamins and minerals are components of food necessary for the growth and function of the brain and body. They are distributed in all foods in varying amounts and a diverse diet helps provide all these key nutrients.

The 'B complex' vitamins are especially important for the brain and have key roles in producing energy. Vitamins A, C and E are powerful antioxidants and particularly important for promoting and preserving memory in the elderly.

Minerals are important factors in preserving the vigour of the brain. Magnesium and manganese are required for brain energy, and sodium, potassium and calcium are important in nerve cell communication, facilitating the transmission of messages.

Recommended dietary allowances

The recommended dietary allowance, or RDA, is used to define the amount of an individual nutrient that is determined to be adequate to meet the daily nutrient needs of practically all healthy persons. Health departments and science academies in each country around the world determine RDAs for various age groups and for males and females. These figures are used by nutritionists to evaluate the adequacy of diets of groups of people or individuals. However, many countries now recognize that although RDAs may be adequate for the 'average healthy' person, there needs to be further guidelines for people who may have greater needs for various nutrients. As a consequence, many countries now publish groups of figures recommending ranges of nutrient values. For example, the Food and Nutrition Board of the National Academy of Sciences in the United States publishes Dietary Reference Intakes (DRIs), while the United Kingdom's Department of Health publishes Dietary Reference Values (DRVs).

Although the RDA figures may vary from country to country, they are basically similar. This book uses RDAs as set out by the European Community.

Working together

In the following chapters, we will be looking at the foods that supply the vast array of nutrients needed by the brain. It is important to remember that each and every nutrient is essential for peak brain performance. We now know that a deficiency in even just one vitamin or mineral can result in lower IQ, mood changes or even depression.

This is because nutrients work together to make things happen in the body and brain. The term 'synergy' is used to describe the process whereby two nutrients working together have the effect of multiplying their benefits for human health. An example of synergy is the way in which vitamins C and E work. Both are antioxidants, which fight free radicals, but vitamin C also recycles the vitamin E, thus allowing it to carry on the fight even longer.

The concept of synergy may seem complicated. However, nature has made it easy for us by providing the nutrients that work together in the same foods. For example, sweet potatoes contain vitamins A, C and E, while cod, lentils and chickpeas are all good sources of both vitamin B6 and zinc.

As we age, the number of nerve cells in our bodies declines and the brain becomes less efficient at making and sending nerve impulses. The result is to slow thinking, cloud understanding and dull memory. However, a diet packed with the key antioxidant nutrients can delay and, in some cases, arrest the decline of mental function in old age.

The body requires high-quality food to make healthy brain cells, and to supply energy for brain power. Thus a nutrient-rich diet is the key to achieving an increased IQ, improving memory function and promoting a more upbeat outlook on life in general.

Recommended ranges of nutrient values

US Dietary Reference Intakes (DRIs)
- ☐ Estimated Average Requirement (EAR) – the requirement defined by a specified indicator of specific group
- ☐ Recommended Dietary Allowance (RDA) – the amount sufficient to meet the nutrient requirements of nearly all individuals in the group
- ☐ Tolerable Upper Intake Level (UL) – the maximum level that is unlikely to pose risks of adverse health effects to almost all of the individuals in the group

UK Dietary Reference Values (DRVs)
- ☐ Lower Reference Nutrient Intake (LRNI) – the level that is enough for only a small number of people with low needs
- ☐ Estimated Average Requirement (EAR) – the 'average' requirement for a nutrient
- ☐ Reference Nutrient Intake (RNI) – the level that is enough for almost every individual, even someone who has high needs for the nutrient
- ☐ Safe Intake – the intake of a nutrient for which there is not enough information to estimate requirements

Supplements

It is essential to eat a nutrient-rich diet in order to achieve the recommended dietary intakes. The recipes in this book are designed to help you achieve adequate consumption of the key brain nutrients. However, many nutritionists also advise taking a good multivitamin and mineral supplement to ensure that your body is getting all the vital nutrients for optimum brain power.

brain boosters

In addition to water, the human brain requires proteins, carbohydrates, fats, vitamins and minerals for peak thinking performance. Each of these key nutrients has a role to play in feeding the brain, and each can be associated with a particular food source in which it is most easily found. Learn how to identify good brain foods and improve your diet with these essential brain-boosting ideas.

What do we mean by good-quality food? Nutritionists encourage the eating of what they call 'nutrient-dense' foods rather than 'empty calories'. Empty calories are those foods, particularly highly processed foods including pastries, biscuits, sweets and chocolates, sugary breakfast cereals, preserved meats and high-fat salty snacks, that can help you meet – or even exceed! – your daily calorie requirements but do not contain the necessary vitamins and minerals needed to encourage mental and physical health.

Good-quality whole foods are the freshest fruits and vegetables, crisp salads, fresh fish and naturally reared poultry and meat, whole grains, nuts, seeds and pulses.

All foods contain some protein, fat and carbohydrates, plus an assortment of vitamins and minerals. For instance, although chicken, fish and beef are predominantly protein foods, they still contain small amounts of carbohydrates; and although brown rice supplies lots of carbohydrates it still contains some protein, vitamins and minerals. Vegetables and fruits supply lots of vitamins and minerals in a primarily carbohydrate base.

Proteins: complete and incomplete

Protein is needed to build the brain's messengers – the neurotransmitters. During digestion, protein is broken down into smaller units called amino acids. These are the basic building blocks for all body tissues and, most significantly, for the neurotransmitters. The body requires approximately 22 amino acids but can make most of these from a few essential amino acids: leucine, isoleucine, lysine, tryptophan, threonine, methionine, phenylalanine and valine.

You can think of amino acids as letters of the alphabet. The different combinations of letters make words that can be strung together to make the sentences or mental messages. Two amino acids, tyrosine and tryptophan, are vital for making key

neurotransmitters, which regulate mood and lift depression. Tyrosine and tryptophan are found in dairy products, eggs, oats and turkey meat.

In order for the body to use amino acids properly, all the eight essential amino acids must be present at the same time and in the correct proportions. If just one essential amino acid is low or missing, then the body cannot make any of the other necessary amino acids. This is rather like trying to write a sentence without all the letters to use.

Food proteins are classified as either 'complete' or 'incomplete', based on whether they contain all the essential amino acids. For instance most meats, fish and dairy products contain all eight so they are called complete proteins, whereas grains, vegetables and fruits are incomplete protein foods because they contain very low amounts or are missing one of the essentials. These incomplete protein foods need to be combined together to provide all the essential amino acids in the right ratios. Wheat products are deficient in the amino acid lysine but contain lots of methionine, whereas the reverse is true for beans. A complete protein can therefore be provided in a meal that combines beans with corn, nuts, rice, seeds or grains.

This does not necessarily mean that complete proteins are better than vegetable combinations in providing amino acids. Meat, eggs and dairy

Complementary proteins

Vegetarians and vegans in particular need to focus on the right food combinations in order to ensure they are getting all the essential amino acids. Some 'complete' protein combinations are:
- ☐ Legumes or fresh vegetables combined with grains, pasta or brown rice. Authentic recipe examples are Native American succotash (maize and beans), South American refried beans and tortillas, and dhal and chapatis from India
- ☐ Sesame seeds or brazil nuts with fresh vegetables
- ☐ Lentils or beans with any types of nut

Amino acids

Nutritionists use the word 'essential' to describe those nutrients that must be consumed in the diet because the human body cannot make them internally.

Essential amino acids
The following amino acids are considered 'essential' for life:
- ☐ Isoleucine
- ☐ Leucine
- ☐ Lysine
- ☐ Methionine
- ☐ Phenylalanine
- ☐ Threonine
- ☐ Tryptophan
- ☐ Valine

'Semi-essential' amino acids
These are so-called because although they can be made by the adult body, babies, young children and perhaps the very ill may not be able to make enough for their needs and so require a dietary supply:
- ☐ Arginine
- ☐ Histidine

products, although supplying all the vital amino acids, are also high in saturated fats and consuming large quantities of these may be undesirable. The best advice is to eat a wide variety of all the complete and incomplete protein foods to ensure an adequate supply of the amino acids needed to promote mental health.

Carbohydrates: slow- or fast-releasing

During the digestion of food, carbohydrates in the food are broken down into smaller, simple sugar molecules such as fructose, galactose and glucose (also called dextrose). Fructose is found naturally in honey and in plants; galactose in milk. Glucose occurs naturally in many different fruits and vegetables. It is the body and the brain's favourite fuel as it helps to maintain concentration, promote alertness and provide the power for all the brain's activities.

It is vital for the health and function of the brain that it receives a constant and even supply of glucose from the blood circulating around the body. Ideally, there should be the equivalent of between one and two teaspoons of this sugar dissolved in the blood stream at all times. This glucose in the blood can then be converted into the energy that feeds the muscles in the body and also fuels the brain.

Balancing blood sugar

As soon as carbohydrate foods are digested, glucose is released into the bloodstream. Slow-releasing carbohydrates are found in brown rice, wholegrain pasta, dark rye bread and fruits and vegetables; these foods are more 'complex' than refined or sugary foods and contain more fibre, which helps to slow down the release of the sugar.

Fast-releasing carbohydrates are found in sweets, honey, sugary cereals and white bread and consist of easily digestible sugars. These carbohydrate foods are more refined and break down into glucose fairly quickly, flooding the blood with too much sugar. This is not desirable since the rapid conversion to glucose means that the body and the brain receive an uncomfortable jolt of energy. These surges are often followed by dramatic drops in glucose delivery, resulting in decreased energy, shorter attention span and an inability to concentrate.

Fluctuations in blood sugar are responsible for the mid-morning and mid-afternoon sweet craving. Many people often have trouble working without a cup of tea or coffee and a biscuit at these times between meals.

In some cases, a drop in blood sugar level can make normal brain function difficult, and people may experience wide-ranging effects including irritability, nervousness, depression, crying spells, panic attacks, anxiety, confusion, forgetfulness and hyperactivity. Some people have headaches, palpitations, dizziness, vertigo, fatigue and insomnia when their blood sugar levels drop.

Tips

In order to maintain an even supply of glucose flowing to the brain:

Always eat breakfast. Choose porridge oats or wholemeal toast with a poached egg rather than a sugary cereal

Eat small frequent meals, which contain protein plus slow-releasing carbohydrates; protein counteracts the effects of carbohydrate

Avoid sugar and sweets

Avoid fast-releasing carbohydrates such as processed breakfast cereals, cakes made with white flour, and white rice

Avoid caffeine in coffee, tea and cola drinks

Avoid alcohol

Avoid, or at least reduce, cigarettes

Reduce stress

Eat complex carbohydrates found in wholegrain bread, brown rice and vegetables

Exercise regularly

Refined foods are not the only cause of fluctuations in the amount of sugar in the blood. Stress, caffeine, alcohol and smoking can all artificially raise blood sugar levels and cause the body to go through the rebalancing process, often resulting in the same problems.

It is important for the diet to include plenty of complex, slow-releasing carbohydrate foods, such as millet, whole wheat, rye, brown rice, corn, plus beans, fresh fruits and vegetables to provide all the key brain-boosting vitamins and minerals.

Fats: saturated and essential

In our 'fat phobic' culture, the idea that fats have significant health roles may be difficult to understand. It is true that most fats in the diet are totally unnecessary and in some cases harmful to health. However, there are some fats, called essential fatty acids which are just that – essential!

Fats, also called lipids, are made from fatty acids. Fatty acids come in different lengths and degrees of saturation. Fatty acids are composed of carbon, hydrogen and oxygen atoms strung together in a long chain. When hydrogen atoms occupy all the available binding sites in the chain, it is called a saturated fat because it is 'saturated' with the hydrogen atoms. Saturated fats ('hard' fats) are usually hard or solid

at room temperature and are found in animal products, for example in meat, cheese and butter. In monounsaturated fats, one hydrogen atom is missing. These fatty acids are found in olive oil and are liquid at room temperature. Polyunsaturated fatty acids (PUFAs) have several hydrogen atoms missing along the chain and are found in fish and plant oils. Essential fatty acids are polyunsaturated.

The body has no nutritional need for saturated fats. In fact, saturated fats have been associated with increased risk of obesity, strokes and cardiovascular disease. A diet high in saturated fats can cause artery walls to thicken, reducing the flow of blood carrying vital nutrients and oxygen to the brain.

Essential fats are liquid at room temperature. There are two key essential fatty acids – called omega-6 oils and omega-3 oils. Omega-6 oils are found in nuts and seeds, while omega-3 oils are found in oily fish. These fats are important because they are vital for both the structure of the nervous system – the brain is more than 60 per cent fat – and the function of mental activities. Intelligence and brain performance depend on the number of connections between neurons or nerve cells. At the point where nerve cells touch each other is a layer of essential fats. A diet high in these essential fatty acids improves learning by guaranteeing good transmission of messages between cells.

Vitamins and minerals

The body cannot manufacture most vitamins itself so it is important to get these from food. Some are co-factors, which means that the vitamins work together with proteins, fats and carbohydrates to perform important functions. Vitamins help to manufacture enzymes. Enzymes 'make things happen' in the body – everything from digesting food to making neurotransmitters.

The group of vitamins called 'B complex' are especially important for the brain. These include vitamins B1, B2, B3, B5, B6, B12 and folic acid, which have key roles in producing energy for each and every cell. When someone does not consume enough B vitamins, they may lack energy, feel tired and lethargic, and have trouble concentrating and maintaining alertness.

Vitamins A, C and E are key antioxidants. Anti-oxidants fight chemically active atoms called free radicals, which can cause serious damage to brain cells. Vitamins A, C and E are particularly important for promoting and preserving memory in the elderly. Approximately 17 minerals are thought to be essential to human nutrition. Minerals form parts of bones, teeth, muscle, blood and nerve cells. They are important factors in preserving the vigour of the brain, as well as the heart. In particular, the minerals magnesium and manganese are required to convert carbohydrates into brain energy. Sodium, potassium and calcium are important in cell-to-cell communication and are needed to maintain an efficient nerve network, facilitating the transmission of messages.

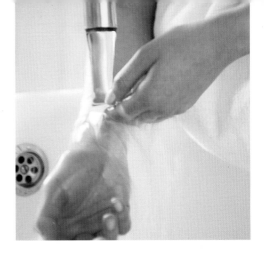

Water

The human body is almost 70 per cent water, so the importance of water is never questioned. Water plays a role in almost every bodily process including digestion, absorption, circulation and excretion. Water in the blood dissolves and transports nutrients throughout the body and to the brain. It also maintains body temperature and carries waste out of the body. Despite this, few people drink enough water and most are confused about the quality of their water.

Tap water is generally obtained from streams, rivers or lakes and collected in reservoirs and underground wells. Most people assume that the water from their tap is clean, safe and healthy. However water is subject to many types of impurities including bacteria, parasites, pesticides, chemicals and toxins.

Chlorine is often added to public water to kill off harmful micro-organisms. Pesticides used in farming can seep into underground water supplies and be fed into homes. Other toxins and metals may also find their way into tap water. Although water suppliers attempt to keep these impurities to a minimum, for sensitive individuals these chemicals may cause headaches, fatigue and depression. Many people are concerned about the potentially harmful effects of consuming this chemical cocktail pouring from the tap.

There are alternatives to tap water. Either you can remove the impurities by using a water filter or you can buy bottled water.

Carbon-type water filters are designed to collect impurities; microfiltration systems made from different materials filter out contaminants; and special ion-exchange resin filters are designed to remove heavy metals. Reverse osmosis and ceramic filters are also considered good, however no filter can remove absolutely every contaminant.

A range of bottled waters is now available in every supermarket, including mineral water, spring water and distilled or deionized water. Some are naturally carbonated, others artificially carbonated and others still. Artificial carbonation, usually labelled 'carbonated natural water' is to be distinguished from naturally carbonated water, labelled 'naturally sparkling water'. Artificial carbonation should be avoided as the added carbon atoms can attach themselves to minerals and carry them out of the body.

How much to drink?

The optimum quantity of water to drink in a day depends on many factors, including the climate and the activities you are involved in. Warm weather and exercise increase the body's need for water. In general, most people should drink 1–2 litres (2–4 pints) a day.

Remember that coffee, tea and alcohol, although liquids, tend to dehydrate you because the body loses water when excreting them. Not only do these drinks not count in the total liquid intake, but they actually increase the need for water.

Dehydration has been shown to contribute to poor concentration and memory in the elderly. Diluted fruit juices, herbal and fruit teas are tasty alternatives to water and will supplement vitamin and mineral supplies at the same time. Also, several portions of fruit and vegetables every day can supply up to 50 per cent of your body's daily needs, then you would only need to drink 1 litre (2 pints) of water a day.

Sources of B vitamins

The neat system of identifying vitamins by letters and numbers has broken down as more have been discovered. Some of the B complex vitamins are known simply by name.

- □ B1 (thiamine) – found in soya beans, brown rice and sunflower seeds
- □ B2 (riboflavin) – found in organ meats, almonds, mushrooms and whole grains
- □ B3 (niacin) – found in legumes, whole grains and avocados
- □ B5 (pantothenic acid) – found in organ meats, brewers' yeast, mushrooms, avocados, egg yolks and whole grains
- □ B6 (pyridoxine) – found in whole grains, legumes, bananas, seeds and nuts
- □ B12 (cobalamine) – found in liver, kidney, meat, fish, eggs and cheese
- □ Folic acid – found in green leafy vegetables, legumes, nuts, liver, eggs and wheatgerm
- □ Biotin – found in nuts, chicken, brewers' yeast and egg yolks
- □ Choline – found in nuts, pulses, citrus fruits, wheatgerm, liver and egg yolks

brain drain

In order for the brain to perform at its peak, it is vital to provide it with a ready supply of the important nutrients described in previous chapters. In practice this may be easier said than done. Firstly, the way in which food is produced, stored and prepared can reduce the nutrient content of food. Secondly, chemicals and other substances in the diet can actually rob the body of nutrients by interfering with their absorption and use. Lastly, some perfectly good, even beneficial, foods may produce an allergic response in some people.

Food production

Every day we are exposed to a plethora of chemicals and pollutants in the air we breathe, the water we drink and the food we eat. Fruits, vegetables and meats all contain chemicals our prehistoric ancestors never had to deal with, either added deliberately by farmers to increase productivity or arriving as contaminants via air, water or soil. The consequences of long-term exposure to tiny amounts of these chemicals is unknown, but recent research suggests that there may be an association between the pesticides used in agriculture and episodes of depression, memory decline, fluctuating moods and aggressive outbursts.

Fruits and vegetables

Many of the pesticides used on fruit and vegetable crops are designed to kill various pests by causing damage to their nerves and brain. What effect these chemicals have on humans is unknown as yet. We do know, however, that in sensitive individuals pesticide residues in food can cause anxiety, hyperactivity, dizziness, blurred vision and muscle weakness. Pesticides can also interact with other chemicals in the body and increase the potential for respiratory and digestive problems. It appears that children are the ones most at risk from pesticide contamination because they are still growing, and it is thought that hyperactivity in some children may be associated with pesticide exposure (see page 38).

The way to avoid pesticide contamination is to go organic. Organically grown vegetables and fruits are not only virtually free from pesticides, they also contain more vitamins and minerals than conventionally grown produce. In particular, they contain more protein and more vitamin C, and more minerals like potassium, calcium, magnesium, iron and manganese. This is because the chemical fertilizers used in intensive farming systems contain only the minimum of a few key minerals required for plant growth. As a result food grows more quickly and the soil eventually becomes

depleted of the other trace elements not included in the commercial fertilizer. Organic farmers, on the other hand, use natural fertilizers. These contain a wide variety of minerals and feed the soil rather than the crop itself, thereby maintaining the natural balance of minerals in the soil.

Organic produce may be a little more expensive, but the additional nutrients and reduced exposure to toxins may be well worth the cost in terms of both human health and the environment.

If organic foods are not available to you, you should remember always to wash fruits and vegetables thoroughly. In particular, green leafy vegetables, like lettuce and cabbage, should be rinsed carefully, leaf by leaf. Root vegetables, such as carrots and parsnips, and fruit such as apples and pears should always be peeled before cooking or eating because many of the pesticide residues are concentrated in the surface layers.

Meat: free-range and organic

The meat debate is not only about the chemical residues that may be found in the meat but also about animal welfare. The conditions under which an animal is kept will affect the health of the animal and ultimately that of the consumer.

In conventionally farmed poultry and livestock the intensive conditions may mean that the animals are kept in crowded conditions. Because these conditions encourage the spread of infections and disease, many animals in intensive farms are routinely fed antibiotics to prevent illness. Some farmers claim to use antibiotics only when absolutely necessary. However, given the often crowded conditions this may be more often than desired and some experts fear that the regular use of antibiotics may encourage the growth of more resistant micro-organisms.

In addition, the processed feed used in conventional farming is most likely to have been made from crops grown intensively with the use of pesticides and then treated with preservatives. It is possible that some chemicals in the animal feed may find their way to the supermarket shelves.

The term 'free-range' is primarily about animal welfare and health. In the case of chickens, free-range means that each bird is guaranteed a minimum of indoor and outdoor space. In conventional farming, the birds live in more crowded conditions, which may have health implications for the chickens, requiring more frequent use of antibiotics.

The term 'organic' refers to the food the animal is fed. Organic livestock and chickens, in addition to being raised outdoors, are given organic feed. The animals are not fed antibiotics so they develop natural resistance to disease.

In some countries, cattle are given steroid hormones to promote growth. Whether these steroids are still present in the meat when it is sold in supermarkets and whether they could have any effect on the consumer is still under debate.

In general, it is unclear what effects long-term exposure to small doses of antibiotics, pesticides and other chemicals have on the health of the human brain and body, but it seems likely that these effects will eventually emerge. Again, organic and free-range poultry and meats may be more expensive but if you think of their purchase as an investment in your family's future health you will probably consider them well worth the extra money.

Processing and refining

When foods are refined or processed in any way they lose many important vitamins and minerals. It is important to remember that flour, both white and brown, is usually sold as 'fortified' flour, which means that vitamins and minerals have been added back in after it has been milled. Wholemeal usually has higher levels of nutrients than the fortified white or brown varieties. Compared with fortified white, wholemeal flour has six times the magnesium, double the potassium and iron, almost five times the zinc, twelve times the selenium, four times the vitamin E and 50 per cent or more B vitamins. It is better to use wholegrain pasta and brown rice rather than the white varieties, and you could also try introducing some more unusual grains like millet and quinoa.

When molasses, a natural syrup extracted from sugar cane, is refined to make white sugar, all the vitamins B1, B2, B3, B5, B6, folic acid, copper and magnesium are lost. This loss is compounded by the fact that the body needs to use its stores of these same vitamins in order to breakdown the sugar in the first place. So not only does consuming white sugar provide very little vitamins or minerals, it depletes the body's reserves as well. Brown sugar and molasses are far more nutritious ways of sweetening foods and drinks.

Storage

Storing food for a long time can also contribute to nutrient loss. Vitamin C is particularly vulnerable to air, heat and light and it rapidly deteriorates during transporting and storage. A sliced cucumber left standing for just 3 hours will lose almost 50 per cent of its vitamin C content, while a sliced cantaloupe left uncovered can lose 35 per cent of its vitamin C in less than 24 hours. Even fruits and vegetables that have not been cut open can lose important vitamins and minerals over time.

If you are lucky enough to have access to locally grown produce – or indeed can grow some of your own fruit and vegetables in the garden – you will know just how long it has been stored. If it is freshly harvested it is likely to have a higher nutrient content than food that has been transported from far away. Many foods these days are flown in from other parts of the world and may have been refrigerated and stored for many weeks or even months before they reach the supermarket shelves. And of course fruit and vegetables bought when they are in season in your part of the world will almost always be freshest.

Having bought the freshest produce you can find, do not then make the mistake of leaving it lying around in your kitchen cupboard for a week. Keep fresh fruits and vegetables in a cool, dark place in order to preserve valuable flavonoids (nutrients responsible for the natural colour of fruit and vegetables), and store other foods according to the recommendations on the packet.

How best to cook

Nutritionists are undecided about the benefits of eating raw versus cooked foods. On the one hand, cooking can easily destroy key vitamins and minerals; on the other hand, cooking makes some nutrients easier to digest and absorb.

Part of the role of the digestion process is to break down the individual cell walls of the food and release the vital nutrients from within. Cooking, puréeing and mashing all work to break down these cells' walls and to prepare them for the body's digestive processes. If foods are to be eaten raw, it is important to make sure they are washed thoroughly first. You should also remember that raw fruit and vegetables should be chewed thoroughly. This will start the breakdown process and will help to release nutrients so that they can be absorbed by the digestive tract and delivered to the brain.

The disadvantage of cooking is that heat of any type destroys most nutrients, the degree of destruction depending on how long the food is cooked and how hot the temperature. Ideally, food should be cooked for as short a time as possible at the lowest temperature possible. The exceptions to this are, of course, meat, fish and eggs, when it is important to reach temperatures high enough to kill off any harmful micro-organisms.

Frying produces the highest temperatures and should be avoided as much as possible. Frying can turn essential fatty acids into harmful chemicals called free radicals. If frying cannot be avoided, use butter or olive oil and fry for as short a time as possible. Grilling cooks food at lower temperatures so is less destructive than frying. However, it is important to avoid burning food, which also produces free radicals.

Boiling food in large saucepans of water can destroy water-soluble vitamins and minerals as the nutrients leach out into the water and are then thrown away. It is better to cook vegetables by steaming them lightly, using a small amount of water. Do not cut the vegetables up too small, which will allow nutrients to flow out of the cut surfaces. Steaming large chunks will keep the temperature at the centre of the food as low as possible, and will preserve the nutrient content there.

Food that is microwaved is cooked in its own water. This has the advantage of avoiding nutrients leaching out of the food. However, the temperatures reached in microwaves will destroy many nutrients. Thus, in reality, lightly steaming vegetables for the shortest length of time will maintain the highest levels of nutrients while helping to break down the cell walls, and thereby releasing important brain-building nutrients. If you do not have a steamer, you can always steam food in a colander set over a pan of boiling water or even just use a small amount of water and keep an eye on it to make sure it does not boil dry.

Did you know?

- [ ] During milling, wheat loses 77 per cent of vitamin B1, 80 per cent of B2, 81 per cent of B3, 72 per cent of B6, 50 per cent of B5, 67 per cent of folic acid, and 86 per cent of the vitamin E.
- [ ] Vegetables that are boiled will have lost 20–50 per cent of their B vitamins, 50 per cent of their vitamin C and 20 per cent of their mineral content.

Nutrient robbers

A diet of fresh, nutrient-rich, well-prepared foods may still not provide enough nourishment to boost brain power. Certain lifestyle factors, pollutants and even foods can actually rob the body of important vitamins and minerals. Anti-nutrients are foods and drinks that steal nutrients from the body in various ways. Either they prevent a nutrient from being absorbed by attaching to it and carrying it out of the body, or they use excessive amounts of an important nutrient, preventing it from doing its good work in the brain. Examples are refined sugar, alcohol and caffeine.

Grains

A substance called phytic acid found in grains can interfere with the absorption of many minerals, including calcium, magnesium and zinc. These minerals are all vital for good memory and concentration. Although bread, pasta and cereals are good foods to eat, you should avoid having them at every meal.

Smoking

It is well known that smoking causes many serious health problems, but its association with a reduction in brain power is less widely recognized.

Take a break

The amount of caffeine in your morning cup will depend on how strongly it is made. Most nutritionists recommend no more than 100 mg of caffeine a day. The amounts of caffeine listed below are for a 150 ml (¼ pint) cup of common caffeinated drinks:

Filtered coffee	110–150 mg
Percolated coffee	60–125 mg
Instant coffee	40–105 mg
Tea	20–100 mg
Cola drinks	20 mg
Hot chocolate	10 mg

Chocolate also contains a high level of caffeine. For example, one slice of chocolate cake contains around 20–30 mg caffeine.

Researchers at the University of London recently reported that smoking increased the risk of impaired cognitive ability in a group of 889 men and women aged 65 or older.

Smoking depletes all the B vitamins required for mental energy. It also increases the need for vitamin C, robbing the brain of this vital nutrient, which acts to protect brain cells from free radical activity and thus to preserve memory.

Junk foods

Highly processed 'junk foods' contain many additives and preservatives thought to be detrimental to the health of brain and body. Many have high levels of sugar, salt and fats. By the age of 18 many children are likely to have eaten their own body weight in food additives. Some of these additives trigger hyperactivity in susceptible children, as well as causing rashes and asthma. The refined sugar in junk foods raises blood sugar levels temporarily, leading to fluctuations in the supply of energy to the brain. These can reduce the ability to

---

What's wrong with junk foods?

- Usually high in sugar – can cause fluctuations in blood sugar levels and inconsistent energy supplies to the brain
- High in artificial sweeteners – may be linked with behavioural problems
- Usually high in saturated fats – too much stops blood delivering nutrients to the brain
- Tend to be low in vitamins and minerals
- Fizzy drinks are high in phosphorus – can interfere with the absorption of calcium, which is vital for the neuromessengers of the brain
- Usually high in additives – colourings, flavourings, preservatives

concentrate and shorten the attention span, especially in children. However, drinks and foods labelled 'sugar-free' contain artificial sweeteners such as aspartame and saccharin, which have been linked with behavioural problems.

Manufacturers often use saturated fats in processed foods to improve the flavour. These harmful fats tend to clog arteries and reduce blood flow to the brain. Hydrogenated fats hinder the absorption of essential fats needed to maintain the structure of the brain's nerve cells.

Fizzy or carbonated drinks are high in phosphorus which interferes with calcium absorption. It is important that the balance between phosphorus and calcium is maintained. However, since phosphorus is found in most foods there tends to be too much in the diet rather than too little and the excess prevents calcium from being absorbed. Calcium is vital for the production of neuro-transmitters and when these minerals are out of balance, neurotransmitters are less efficient at communicating their messages.

Food allergies

More and more people say that they are 'allergic', 'sensitive' or 'intolerant' to this or that food. But what does this really mean and how can this lead to poor physical and mental health?

Some symptoms and conditions that may be related to food sensitivity include depression, anxiety, hyperactivity in children, poor mental concentration, brain fog, fatigue, apathy, headache or migraine, fluid retention, muscle aches, excessive mucus and catarrh, diarrhoea, constipation, abdominal bloating, irritable bowel syndrome, eczema and weight gain.

In general, conventional medicine recognizes only those relatively rare food allergies that produce an acute, severe and immediate reaction. For example, many people are allergic to peanuts – even small traces in foods can cause them to come out in a rash or, in more serious cases, to develop the severe, life-threatening reaction called anaphylactic shock.

There is, however, another type of food allergy for which the scientific evidence is mounting. In many people, certain foods can trigger an array of symptoms, which can appear hours or even days after eating the offending food. It can sometimes be difficult to identify exactly which food is the culprit, and conventional allergy tests often seem inadequate at identifying these allergens. There are a variety of food allergy tests available but many nutrition practitioners consider the 'elimination challenge test' to be the most accurate way of

testing for food sensitivities. Furthermore, it is inexpensive as well.

The idea is simple: remove the suspected foods from the diet for a period of time, see if the symptoms disappear and then reintroduce the foods and monitor carefully whether the symptoms return. Taking a pulse count when reintroducing the food may also help to identify offending foods.

In very sensitive individuals and children, the reintroduction of a food allergen may cause an extreme reaction. This is an important consideration if the person has experienced profound allergic reactions in the past. If the original symptoms were severe and the improvement upon eliminating the food quite marked, then you may wish to consult your healthcare provider for advice before reintroducing the food and risking a severe reaction. Common food allergens (foods that cause an allergic reaction) are wheat, gluten grains (wheat, rye, oats and barley), dairy products, coffee, tea, nuts, citrus fruit and soya products. Often a person will feel a strong need to eat the food – almost an addiction.

Some food reactions may be caused when food that is only partially digested passes from the intestines into the bloodstream. When this happens the body mounts an immune reaction and there is enormous potential for a variety of physical and mental reactions. Stress, alcohol and infections can increase the body's propensity to allow these undigested food particles into the bloodstream so it is important to chew food completely to help start the digestive process.

Caution

Upon eliminating a food from the diet some people experience withdrawal symptoms such as headaches, feeling hungry, nervousness, inability to concentrate and insomnia. These feelings usually last only a few days and are in general an indication that you are on the right track.

Elimination challenge test

Step 1
Decide which foods you think may be causing your symptoms. Remember, these will usually be foods that you eat frequently (5+ times a week). Often you will almost feel addicted to the food and 'need' to eat it.

Step 2
Eliminate the suspected food from the diet for 28 days (for children no more than 7–10 days). Some people prefer to eliminate only one food type at a time, while others may want to avoid two or three suspected foods. During this time, make a note of any lessening of symptoms or improvement in mood or concentration.

Step 3
At the end of the 28 days, sit down for 5 minutes then take your pulse for 1 minute. The best way to do this is to find your carotid artery. This is located just below your jaw in the groove where your head and neck meet, on either side of your wind pipe. Use your index and middle finger tips to feel around in the groove for a tangible pulsation. Using a watch with a second hand, count how many times you feel your pulse beat during a 60-second period.

Step 4
Eat a regular portion of the food that was eliminated. It is best to eat the food in its purest form rather than mixed with other foods. For example, if you have given up dairy products for four weeks, it is better to introduce a lump of cheese rather than a cheese sandwich.

Step 5
Take your pulse again after 10, 30 and 60 minutes.
- □ If your pulse goes up by more than 10 beats per minute at any time during the hour after eating the food, then it is likely that this food is responsible for mental and/or physical symptoms.
- □ If your pulse does not increase but you experience tiredness, headaches, depression, hyperactivity or digestive problems during the following 48 hours, this food may still be responsible for the symptoms.
- □ If your pulse does not increase and you do not experience any particular symptoms, then this food is probably not contributing to symptoms.

Step 6
If you gave up more than one food, wait 48 hours after reintroducing the first food before repeating the above steps with the next food.

Even if this test shows some sensitivity to a particular food, it does not mean that you cannot ever eat this food again. The best course of action is to omit the food for a period of a couple of months, then try reintroducing again according to the above instructions. If there is no observable reactions or pulse increase, then reintroduce the food back into the diet. But be careful not to start eating the food every day as the original symptoms are likely to gradually reappear after time.

Allergen-free diets

One of the difficulties of allergy testing is not so much the difficulty in removing foods from your diet but what to replace them with. You will find that there are tasty alternatives to some common allergen foods (see the ideas opposite for alternatives to dairy products and foods containing gluten).

Gluten and dairy alternatives

Gluten and dairy products in the diet are the most likely causes of food sensitivities. There are some easily available alternative foods.

Gluten can be found in wheat, rye, oats and barley and foods that should be avoided are: most cereals, bread, pasta, pizza, biscuits and cakes. Gluten-free alternatives include: rice or corn cereals, rice-based products such as rice noodles, rice cakes and rice pasta, polenta, corn bread, millet, quinoa, buckwheat and 'gluten-free' labelled products.

Dairy products as a group are easy to identify. Foods that should be avoided are: milk (full, semi-skimmed and skimmed), cheese, yogurt, butter and milk chocolate. Dairy-free alternatives include: soya milk/cheese/yogurt, rice milk/cheese, oat milk and non-dairy spreads such as tahini and nut butters.

dairy-free menus

MENU ONE
breakfast
porridge made with soya or rice milk

lunch
omelette (no cheese or milk) with
  peas and tomatoes

dinner
Brown Rice with Tomato and Red
  Pepper Sauce without Cheese
  (*see page 51*)
or Lamb Steak with Italian and Green
  Beans (*see page 57*)
Blueberry and Blackberry Yogurt
  Syllabub made with soya yogurt
  (*see page 82*)

snacks
crudites, with hummus

MENU TWO
breakfast
corn flakes or puffed rice with soya
  or rice milk

lunch
Mango and Avocado Salad with
  Smoked Chicken (*see page 97*)

dinner
Brazil Nut and Sunflower Seed
  Savoury Cakes (*see page 54*)
or Spiced Mackerel with Celeriac
  Mash (*see page 79*)
fruit, or fruit salad with soya yogurt

snacks
Pumpkin Seed and Muesli Soda
  Bread (*see page 58*)

gluten-free menus

MENU ONE
breakfast
scrambled egg with slice of Pumpkin Seed and Muesli Soda Bread (*see page 58*)

lunch
Bright Red Pepper Soup (*see page 46*)

dinner
Mushrooms with Millet Spaghetti (*see page 95*)
mixed salad or steamed vegetables
Poached Guava with Yogurt Brûlée (*see page 101*)

snacks
Walnut and Sunflower Seed Snacks (*see page 59*)

MENU TWO
breakfast
porridge made with millet or quinoa flakes

lunch
Thick Carrot Soup with Orange and Ginger (*see page 74*)

dinner
Sweet Potato and Spinach Mash with Grilled Cod (*see page 76*)
or Sardines with Spinach Pesto and Roasted Pumpkin (*see page 78*)
mixed salad or steamed vegetables
Black Grape Jelly with Citrus Fruit (*see page 81*)

snacks
Mid-morning Break 'n' Shake (*see page 73*)

MENU THREE
breakfast
gluten-free muesli with semi-skimmed or soya milk plus grated apple

lunch
Beetroot, Sugar Snap and Buckwheat Pasta with Crème Fraîche (*see page 48*)

dinner
Griddled Liver and Bacon with Grilled Potatoes (*see page 94*)
or Red Pesto Turkey and Chickpea Mash (*see page 115*)
Poached Cherries with Almond Milk Pudding (*see page 80*)

snacks
Fig and Molasses Cake Bars (*see page 61*)

food for thought

There is much controversy surrounding the concept of intelligence. Some people insist that intelligence is genetically programmed, something we are born with, while others suggest that intelligence can be fostered within an encouraging educational environment. Now a growing body of scientific evidence suggests that diet can play a key role in improving IQ levels. Students of all ages should assess their diet to ensure that their brain is receiving the correct nutrients.

We have already seen that a large number of different vitamins and minerals are required to produce optimum thinking power. In addition to these nutrients, the body needs carbohydrates, protein and essential fats for proper brain function. Foods that supply these key groups of brain-boosting nutrients are vital for improving concentration and learning ability. For students of any age, eating the right types of foods can lead to a dramatic improvement in health and mental performance.

Brain power

First and foremost, the brain needs energy. Although the brain weighs only 1.5 kg (3 lb), it consumes 25 per cent of the body's total energy. This energy is used to fuel the steady transmission of electrical impulses and communication between nerve cells. Unlike other organs, the brain does not store energy, so in order to function it needs a constant supply of two major fuels: oxygen and glucose. Oxygen is supplied through breathing and the glucose, which is a sugar, is found in carbohydrate foods in the diet. Having a good supply of the correct fuel is vital for peak mental performance.

Fuel for thought

It is important for the brain that the blood delivers a steady and even supply of glucose during studying and periods of intense concentration. Many students complain that in an exam situation, their mind goes blank and they cannot remember a thing. In many cases, it may be that their brains are low on glucose fuel, resulting in poor concentration, reduced mental energy and diminished alertness. The best foods for supplying brain fuel are complex carbohydrates found in whole grains and vegetables.

Many young students consume vast quantities of refined carbohydrates, including sweets, biscuits, chocolates and soft drinks. A survey of British children conducted by the United Kingdom's Ministry of Agriculture, Fisheries and Food (MAFF) in 2000 reported: 'The foods most commonly consumed by young people in the survey, eaten by more than 80 per cent of the group during the seven-day dietary recorded, were white bread, savoury snacks, potato chips (French fries), biscuits, boiled, mashed and jacket potatoes and chocolate confectionery.' Although all these foods contain lots of sugar, it is not the best kind of sugar for the brain. The first important step in achieving academic excellence is to eat what are known as complex carbohydrates, found in fruits and vegetables, seeds, nuts and whole grains in the form of wholemeal and millet pasta, brown rice and quinoa.

Mental messengers

Protein is another important brain food. Via various biochemical steps, proteins are converted to neurotransmitters. These neurotransmitters are the way in which the brain processes information. Key protein foods include meat, fish, eggs and dairy products, such as milk and cheese. Since saturated fats can actually interfere with how the brain's messengers communicate, fish and lean cuts of meat and poultry are the proteins of choice for the smart students.

Smart fats

Omega-3 and omega-6 essential fatty acids are vital for healthy nerve and brain cells. The fats are necessary for proper brain development and function, and have been shown to increase brain size and aid learning. Oily fish (mackerel, herrings, sardines and kippers) are the best sources of omega-3 oils, while fresh brazil nuts, hazelnuts, almonds, sesame seeds and sunflower seeds all contain omega-6 oils.

IQ-boosting minerals and vitamins

The remaining IQ-boosting nutrients are the vitamins and minerals. These are needed in much smaller amounts than carbohydrate or protein foods but each one is vital. Researchers have found that a deficiency in just one of these important vitamins and minerals can reduce mental alertness. A diet rich in fruits, vegetables, whole grains, plus some meat and fish can provide all the key minerals and vitamins needed for mental and physical health.

The nine key minerals necessary for maximum mental powers are: iron, magnesium, phosphorus, manganese, sodium, potassium, calcium, zinc and boron. These nutrients make sure that brain messages travel smoothly around the brain and nervous system. This means increased alertness, greater understanding and improved memory.

It may be boron, but...

In 1998 the US Department of Agriculture reported decreased electrical activity in the brains of subjects given a diet low in boron. The researchers found that boron deficiency resulted in poorer performance in mental tasks and dexterity, attention and short-term memory.

By far the best sources of boron are vegetables, and it is also found in nuts, apples and dried fruits.

Researchers at the Faculty of Medicine, University of the State of Mexico, conducted a study on iron-deficient children between six and twelve years old. They found that iron-deficient (but not anaemic) children had significantly lower scores in tests on information and comprehension, as well as lower overall IQ scores, when compared with children with adequate iron levels.

Worryingly, vitamin and mineral deficiencies are much more prevalent than many people believe. A survey of British children conducted by MAFF in 2000 shows that up to 50 per cent of girls between the ages of 11 and 14 years old get less than the recommended dietary allowance (RDA) for iron. The survey also reports alarmingly low levels of zinc in at least 10 per cent of all children between the ages of 4 and 19, with the figure rising to over 30 per cent for girls aged 11–14. Half of the girls in the 11–14 age bracket were not getting the recommended level of magnesium, a mineral vital for converting carbohydrates to brain glucose fuel.

The recommended intake levels of minerals set by governments may be inadequate for optimum mental and physical performance. The recommendations are designed to avoid signs of deficiency, like anaemia in the case of iron. But as we can see from the Mexico study above, students with low levels of iron experienced learning difficulties even though the levels were not low enough to cause anaemia.

In addition to minerals, there are seven vitamins that are especially important for the brain. These are the B complex vitamins B1, B2, B3, B5, B6 and biotin, plus vitamin C, which are necessary to convert carbohydrates to glucose for mental energy. They are also important in the production of neurotransmitters. The MAFF study reports that only 20 per cent of 15–18-year-old girls eat citrus fruit – a rich source of vitamin C.

Hyperactivity

This central nervous system disorder causes various learning and behavioural problems. The hyperactive child is fidgety, disruptive, aggressive and impulsive and has poor grades at school, often in spite of average or above-average IQ. Although the precise underlying cause is not known, links between diet and hyperactivity have emerged.

Simple changes in diet can often result in remarkable improvements. Adopt a diet high in good-quality protein such as fish and lean meats, avoid refined carbohydrates and choose wholemeal bread and brown rice instead. In addition:

☐ Eliminate all foods with preservatives, artificial colourings and flavourings. Even trace amounts may cause a reaction.
☐ Avoid fizzy and carbonated drinks. Replace with vegetable juices and bottled water.
☐ Test for and avoid any identified food allergies (see page 31). Most common food allergens in hyperactive children are red, yellow and blue dyes, colourings and preservatives, cow's milk, soya, chocolate, grapes, oranges, peanuts, wheat, corn, tomato, eggs, cane sugar, apples, fish and oats.

Variety for health

The best way to incorporate all these essential brain-boosting nutrients into your diet is to eat as wide a range of foods as possible. The key word is variety. Both the person who has a tuna sandwich every single lunchtime and the child who eats only carrots will be missing out on important brain-building vitamins and minerals. Varying the foods you consume could make all the difference to your performance.

Flavonoids

A good general guideline for choosing which vegetable to eat is to look at the colour, which will give you important clues as to its content. There is a group of important nutrients found in plants called phytochemicals. The interesting phytochemicals are called flavonoids and these are responsible for developing the natural colour pigments found in fruits and vegetables. The name flavonoid comes from the Latin flavus, meaning yellow, hence, foods rich in flavonoids are often yellow in colour.

Over 800 varieties of flavonoids have been identified, and many are found as companions to vitamin C. Examples of flavonoids include quercitin in cranberries, rutin in buckwheat, hesperidin from citrus and pycnogenol from pine bark. It is believed that they work with vitamin C in some, as yet unknown, way to protect cell structures from the damage caused by free radicals. Flavonoids are relatively stable and are resistant to heat, oxygen and dryness, although they are destroyed by light. This is why it is a good idea to keep brightly coloured fruits and vegetables, which are rich in flavonoids, stored in a dark, cool place to preserve their precious ingredients.

So, not only does the use of a variety of different coloured fruits and vegetables offer the benefit of attractive-looking dishes, it can also offer a diet that tastes good and provides maximum protection to brain and nerve cells.

Food in technicolour

Fruits and vegetables in natural yellows, reds and greens are likely to be full of nutrients important for a healthy brain:

- ☐ Red pepper
  The red colour is due to the presence of high levels of beta-carotene

- ☐ Onion
  The yellow comes from anthoxanthins, powerful protectants against free-radical damage

- ☐ Broccoli
  Rich in beta-carotene, also evident in carrots – without it broccoli would be a much lighter green

- ☐ Beetroot
  Purple coloration is caused by anthocyanidins, known to protect brain cell membranes

- ☐ Tomato
  Coloured red because of the strong antioxidant lycopene

- ☐ Carrot
  The orange colour comes from beta-carotene, the precursor to vitamin A

Foods in focus

Foods that supply the key groups of nutrients required for optimum brain function can be regarded as IQ-boosters. Recognizing the types of foods you need to eat in order to improve your mental performance could be of great benefit to you.

Red pepper

The red pepper is a ripened version of the green variety and the extra time allowed for maturing increases the overall nutrient content. Both red and green peppers are rich in the protective antioxidant nutrients vitamin C and beta-carotene, which is a vitamin A precursor. However, the red pepper has 20 per cent more vitamin C than the green one and 15 times more beta-carotene. The rich red colour of a red pepper is proof of its high levels of beta-carotene.

Good-quality peppers are fresh, firm and bright in appearance and have a thick flesh. Avoid peppers that are shrivelled, soft or dull in appearance as this is an indication that they may have lost much of their vitamin C. Peppers also contain sodium and potassium, minerals that facilitate the transmission of nerve messages.

Onion

Onions are one of the earliest known foods to be used as a medicine for colds and were in fact thought to be invested with supernatural powers in Ancient Egypt. Their straw-yellow colour comes from the group of flavonoids called anthoxanthins, which boost the immune system and protect vulnerable brain and nerve cells from free-radical damage. The odour of onions is caused by a sulphur-containing oily vapour, which escapes into the air when the onion is cut or peeled. When this volatile oil is inhaled it can cause eyes to sting and water. But the sulphur in onions helps the body to get rid of toxins that can cause cloudy and fuzzy thinking. Onions also stimulate the amino acid activity in the brain and nervous system by helping in the conversion of amino acids to neurotransmitters.

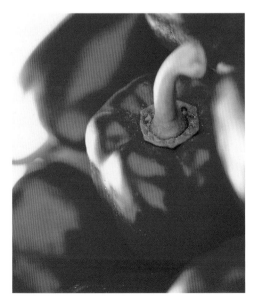

Broccoli

Broccoli, a member of the cabbage family, is an ideal food: it comprises 90 per cent water, it is packed full of vitamins and minerals – and on top of that it contains very few calories. Broccoli is another free-radical fighting food, protecting cells in the brain and body from oxidative damage. The dark green colour manages to disguise the presence of deep orange beta-carotene, but it is in fact the orange colour that makes broccoli dark rather than light green.

In addition to providing a generous supply of flavonoids, broccoli is a rich source of iron, calcium, potassium and vitamin C. A cup of cooked broccoli contains more vitamin C than two oranges. But vitamin C is particularly vulnerable during storage and cooking, so it is best to buy only as much broccoli as you can use immediately or the nutrient levels will decline. When buying broccoli, choose the darkest, greenest stalks on display and cook them only lightly to preserve the precious vitamins in this vegetable.

Beetroot

Beetroot is a bonus brain food because it contains so many important brain nutrients. To produce energy the brain needs carbohydrates plus oxygen. Beetroots are rich in readily usable carbohydrates, and they provide a source of iron (especially useful for vegetarians), which helps blood to carry oxygen to the brain.

The rich purple colour of beetroot is caused by the presence of anthocyanidins. These protect delicate brain cell membranes, making them more receptive to neurotransmitter messages. Beetroots are also rich in the minerals sodium, potassium, calcium and phosphorus, important for good mental health, which all work together to produce and transmit neuromessages.

Fresh and cooked beetroot contain most of the important nutrients; avoid pickled varieties, which are lower in minerals.

When choosing fresh beetroot, look for plump roots that are smooth and firm and avoid those that show any signs of decay.

Beans

Beans are a valuable source of protein, especially for vegetarians. However, because they are moderately low in some of the amino acids, they cannot be considered a 'complete' protein like meat or cheese. However, brown rice, millet pasta or couscous can be used to complement beans to create a nutritious meat substitute.

Beans also supply the synergistic minerals, including magnesium, phosphorus, iron, zinc and manganese, needed to work with the amino acids for constructing the brain's messengers. The rich supply of carbohydrates in beans fuels the brain with the energy to make the whole system work. Note: It is not safe to eat raw or undercooked kidney and soya beans. Follow the manufacturer's instructions regarding cooking.

Tomatoes

The bright red colour of tomatoes is supplied by a phytochemical called lycopene, which is in the same family of carotenoids as the orange-coloured beta-carotene in carrots. Lycopene acts as a powerful antioxidant in protecting the brain and nervous system. Tomatoes contain a wide range of minerals and B vitamins, which help power the brain and produce neuromessengers.

Tomatoes should only be picked when they are ripe and eaten soon after. Unfortunately, today many producers pick the tomatoes when they are too green and then allow them to ripen on their way to the markets. If the seeds or the internal part of the tomato are still green while the outside is red, this is an indication that the fruit has been picked too early. It is best to use the freshest, smallest and reddest tomatoes available as these will be richest in lycopene and vitamin C. However, when fresh tomatoes are not available, canned tomatoes provide suitable backup. They still retain two-thirds of the vitamin C content and one-third of the carotenoid of fresh tomatoes.

Quinoa

Although quinoa has been cultivated in South America since 3000 BC, it is only recently becoming popular elsewhere. Compared with other grains, it is high in protein (16 per cent versus 7.5 per cent in rice), calcium and iron – all key components of neurotransmitters. Calcium is particularly important for calming nerves. Quinoa is also a good source of B vitamins. Since it contains only a very minute quantity of gluten, quinoa is tolerated by most gluten-sensitive individuals.

Nuts and seeds

Nuts and seeds are crammed with lots of smart nutrients. Most importantly, they are rich sources of protein, minerals, as well as omega-6 fatty acids, one of the two groups of 'essential' fatty acids used by the brain to build its messengers (see page 19).

Since each nut and seed has its own unique combination of nutrients it is important to eat a mixture of different ones in order to gain maximum health benefits.

Almonds are the best choice because they are low in saturated fat, rich in omega-6 oils, have plenty of protein and vitamin E, and are particularly rich in calcium (50 g/2 oz almonds contain more calcium than half a cup of milk). Hazelnuts are also a good choice: they have less omega-6 oils than almonds but they have double the amount of manganese than any other nuts.

Brazil and cashew nuts are very high in saturated fats and should be eaten more sparingly. Peanuts, although high in protein, are also high in fats, so are best avoided or eaten in moderation. Walnuts and pumpkin seeds are special as they contain both omega-6 and omega-3 oils (usually found only in oily fish). Sesame seeds contain plenty of zinc, while sunflower seeds are rich in the mineral magnesium and vitamin E.

Most nuts and seeds are also high in undesirable saturated fats – a handful a day can provide the important nutrients without too much fat.

Because nuts contain lots of oil, they can go rancid very easily. It is best to buy them in the shell and crack open as needed. Otherwise, buy nuts and seeds already opened, keep refrigerated and eat while still fresh.

Warning: Some people are very allergic to nuts and seeds, so it is always best to check this before giving someone a nut-containing product.

Molasses

Molasses is a dark, thick, sweet syrup, which is extracted from sugar cane plants. However, unlike white sugar, which contains no vitamins or minerals, molasses is a superfood packed with lots of brain-building nutrients. It has plenty of the minerals – magnesium, iron, copper and manganese – and all the B vitamins required to build and power neurotransmitters. One tablespoon of molasses contains more than three times the iron found in an egg and more calcium than a glass of milk.

Try to add a little molasses to your food every day – to soups, vegetables or meat stews and rich cake mixtures. Try adding a teaspoon or two to a mug of warm milk to make a comforting and rich flavoured drink – ideal in the winter and before going to sleep.

Blackstrap molasses contains more minerals than the light or medium versions and is less sweet. Although not as popular as it once was, it is now readily available from health food stores and can be found in many supermarkets.

Lean meats

The brain requires a good supply of all the amino acids in order to make key neurotransmitters. Only protein-rich foods can supply these amino acids, and since meat contains all eight essential amino acids it is classified as a good-quality 'complete' protein.

The fat portion of meat makes no contribution to human health for either the brain or the body and all the protein is found in the lean muscle. This is why it is important to look for lean meats such as skinless chicken breast. Lamb is higher than chicken in saturated fats but contains three times more iron and five times more zinc than chicken. The general rule of thumb is to buy good-grade lean cuts. In most cuts of lamb, the fat can be easily separated from the lean, hence it can provide the building blocks for neurotransmitters without the fat. In general, even the leanest cuts of beef contain more saturated fats than, say, skinless chicken breasts. So always choose the leanest cuts of beef and remove any visible fat.

Soya bean products

For the vegan, who avoids meat and all animal products like eggs and dairy, tofu provides a good alternative to meat as it is made from soya beans and contains good quantities of all the essential amino acids. However, because tofu contains more water than most meat proteins, larger quantities are required to provide the equivalent protein found in meat. For example, 20 g (¾ oz) protein can be provided by 75 g (3 oz) chicken breast, 175 g (6 oz) lamb or 250 g (8 oz) steamed tofu.

Besides being an excellent source of protein, tofu contains omega-3 oils, phytoestrogens, minerals and vitamins. Most stores now carry a variety of tofu. Silken tofu is smooth and creamy, while the denser, firmer varieties are often smoked or marinated. Tofu is already cooked, so can be eaten as it is or used in cooking.

Other soya bean products include tempeh, which is made from fermented whole soya beans and has a nutty flavour, and miso, a fermented bean paste that is useful for soups and flavourings.

a menu to improve iq

breakfast
scrambled egg on wholemeal granary toast
glass of unsweetened orange juice

lunch
Bright Red Pepper Soup (*see page 46*)
carrot and cucumber sticks
unsweetened fruit juice

dinner
Brown Rice with Tomato and Red Pepper Sauce (*see page 51*)
mixed salad
Almond Milk Jelly with Mango (*see page 62*)

snacks
Fig and Molasses Cake Bars (*see page 61*)
fresh fruit

Bright Red Pepper Soup

A vibrant and warming soup which is ideal for any meal and tastes just as good warm or cold.

2 onions, finely chopped
2 tablespoons groundnut or olive oil
1 garlic clove, crushed (optional)
3 red peppers, deseeded and roughly chopped
2 courgettes, roughly chopped
900 ml (1½ pints) vegetable stock or water
sea salt and freshly ground black pepper

To serve
yogurt or double cream
chopped chives

1 Put the onion in a large saucepan with the oil and gently fry for 5 minutes or until softened and golden brown. Add the garlic, if using, and cook gently for 1 minute.

2 Add the peppers and half the courgettes to the pan. Fry for 5–8 minutes or until softened and brown.

3 Add the stock to the pan with salt and pepper and bring to the boil. Reduce the heat, cover the pan and simmer gently for 20 minutes.

4 When the vegetables are tender blend the mixture, in batches, to a smooth soup and return to the pan. Season to taste, reheat and serve topped with the remaining chopped courgette, yogurt or a swirl of cream and chopped chives.

Serves 4
Preparation time: 15 minutes
Cooking time: 30 minutes

Roasted Onion Soup with Garlic Croûtons

A slowly cooked onion soup is warming and uplifting in the middle of winter. The onions cook to a sweet caramelized flavour, and for the full allium family connection this soup is served with garlic croûtons.

4 large onions, finely chopped
3 tablespoons vegetable or olive oil
1.2 litres (2 pints) vegetable stock
2 teaspoons chopped thyme
1 tablespoon chopped parsley
sea salt and freshly ground black pepper

Garlic croûtons
8–12 thick slices of French or Italian bread
1 small garlic clove, halved
2 tablespoons olive oil
2 tablespoons grated Parmesan or Cheddar
    cheese

1 Put the onion into a large saucepan with the oil. Cook gently for 20 minutes, stirring occasionally.

2 When the onions are very soft and caramelized to a golden brown colour, add the vegetable stock and thyme and bring to the boil. Boil for 2 minutes, reduce the heat, cover and simmer the soup for 30 minutes. Add salt and pepper to taste.

3 Put the mixture into a blender and blend until smooth. Return to the pan and add the parsley. Keep warm while you prepare the croûtons.

4 Lay the thick slices of bread on a baking sheet and toast until they are a golden brown colour.

5 Smear the top of each slice of bread with the cut side of the garlic clove. Drizzle with the olive oil and sprinkle with the Parmesan or Cheddar.

6 Lightly grill the bread slices until the cheese just begins to melt and either serve them with the soup or float one on top of each bowl.

Serves 4
Preparation time: 20 minutes
Cooking time: 1 hour

Beetroot, Sugar Snap and Buckwheat Pasta with Crème Fraîche

Beetroot is an excellent source of many of the major antioxidants.

250 g (8 oz) cooked beetroot
125 g (4 oz) sugar snaps, trimmed and cut
  diagonally into thirds
250 g (8 oz) buckwheat or corn pasta
200 ml (7 fl oz) low fat crème fraîche
2 tablespoons chopped chives
sea salt and freshly ground black pepper
2 tablespoons grated Parmesan cheese, to serve

1 Wearing plastic gloves, peel the beetroot and roughly chop the flesh. Blanch the sugar snaps in boiling water for 1 minute and drain well.

2 Bring a large saucepan of water to the boil. Add the pasta, and cook for 4–5 minutes or until it is soft and cooked through. (Do not overcook wheat-free pasta since it loses its texture easily.) Drain well and return to the pan.

3 Add the beetroot and sugar snaps. Stir over a low heat for 2 minutes until the beetroot is heated through. Remove from the heat, add the crème fraîche and salt and pepper and toss everything together. Add the chopped chives and serve in large bowls topped with grated Parmesan.

Serves 4
Preparation time: 10 minutes
Cooking time: 5–10 minutes

Red Onions Stuffed with Mushrooms and Red Rice

Red onions roast to a sweet flavour and contain toxin-removing quercitin and sulphur amino acid. They are considered highly beneficial for their antiviral and antibiotic properties.

4 large red onions, peeled and left whole
2 tablespoons vegetable or olive oil
125 g (4 oz) button mushrooms, finely chopped
75 g (3 oz) red or brown rice
1 tablespoon chopped parsley
300 ml (½ pint) water
1 tablespoon sultanas (optional)
1 tablespoon freshly grated Parmesan cheese
sea salt and freshly ground black pepper

To serve
extra virgin olive oil
coriander leaves

1 Cut the top off each onion and scoop out the centre using a teaspoon. Finely chop the scooped-out onion. Heat the oil in a frying-pan. Add the chopped onion and gently fry until soft and golden brown. Add the mushrooms and cook for a further 5 minutes, stirring frequently or until the mushrooms are cooked.

2 Meanwhile, bring a large pan of water to the boil. Add the onion 'cups' and simmer for 10 minutes or until they begin to soften, then drain well.

3 Add the red rice, parsley, salt, pepper and water to the mushrooms. Bring to the boil and boil for 5 minutes. Cover the pan and simmer for a further 30 minutes or until the grains are soft. Add extra water if the grains begin to dry out.

4 Preheat the oven to 190°C (375°F) Gas Mark 5. Stir the sultanas into the rice mixture and spoon the mixture into the onions.

5 Put the onions in a roasting tin and cover tightly with foil. Cook in the centre of the preheated oven for 30 minutes. Remove the foil, sprinkle the Parmesan over the top of the onions and cook for a further 10 minutes. Serve drizzled with extra olive oil and topped with coriander leaves.

Serves 4
Preparation time: 30 minutes
Cooking time: 1½ hours

Tomato Ratatouille Gratin

1 Preheat the oven to 220°C (425°F) Gas Mark 7. Put the onions in a large pan with the oil and gently fry until softened and golden brown. Add the garlic, if using, and cook for 1 further minute.

2 Add the aubergine and courgettes to the pan and cook on all sides until softened and beginning to brown. Add the chopped red, yellow and green peppers to the pan. Stir to coat in the oil. Simmer for 5 minutes until the peppers have softened.

3 Add the canned tomatoes and bring to a fast boil. Reduce the heat, add salt, pepper and the dried mixed herbs, half cover the pan with a lid and simmer for 10 minutes.

4 Spoon the ratatouille mixture into a large ovenproof dish and level the top. Mix the breadcrumbs with the Cheddar and Parmesan and sprinkle on top.

5 Bake the ratatouille in the preheated oven for 20–25 minutes or until the breadcrumb mixture is golden brown and bubbling. Serve with a green salad.

Serves 4–6
Preparation time: 15 minutes
Cooking time: 1 hour

2 onions, finely chopped
4 tablespoons olive oil
2 garlic cloves, crushed (optional)
1 aubergine, diced
500 g (1 lb) courgettes, diced
3 red peppers, deseeded and roughly chopped
1 yellow pepper, deseeded and roughly chopped
2 green peppers, deseeded and roughly chopped
2 x 425 g (14 oz) cans organic chopped tomatoes
2 teaspoons dried mixed herbs
50 g (2 oz) dried breadcrumbs
25 g (1 oz) Cheddar cheese, grated
1 tablespoon grated Parmesan cheese
sea salt and freshly ground black pepper

Brown Rice with Tomato and Red Pepper Sauce

250 g (8 oz) brown rice
10 cm (4 in) piece of dried kombu seaweed
 (optional)
4 tablespoons grated Parmesan or Cheddar
 cheese, to serve

Tomato and red pepper sauce
1 onion, finely chopped
2 tablespoons olive oil
1 red pepper, deseeded and chopped
1 green pepper, deseeded and chopped
2 x 425 g (14 oz) cans organic tomatoes
3 tablespoons tomato purée
1 tablespoon dried mixed herbs
6 pitted black olives, chopped (optional)
2 tablespoons chopped basil or parsley
sea salt and freshly ground black pepper

1 Rinse the rice and add to a large pan of water with the kombu, if using. Bring to the boil, then cover the pan, reduce the heat and simmer for 25 minutes or until the rice is soft and cooked through. Drain well and discard the kombu.

2 Meanwhile cook the onion in a separate pan with the oil until soft. Add the red and green peppers and cook for 4–5 minutes more.

3 Add the canned tomatoes, tomato purée and mixed herbs and bring to a fast simmer. Reduce the heat, cover the pan and simmer for 20 minutes.

4 Just before serving add the olives, if using, together with the basil and seasoning to taste. Serve the tomato sauce on top of the freshly cooked rice and sprinkle with grated Parmesan or Cheddar.

Serves 4–6
Preparation time: 10 minutes
Cooking time: 35 minutes

Vegetable Frittata-Stuffed Focaccia

The ideal takeaway sandwich. Frittata also makes an excellent canapé to serve with drinks: cut into small wedges or squares and offer on cocktail sticks with a few olives.

1 onion, roughly chopped
3–4 tablespoons vegetable oil
125 g (4 oz) small salad or waxy potatoes, sliced
1 red pepper, deseeded and chopped
1 green pepper, deseeded and chopped
2 courgettes, sliced or chopped
75 g (3 oz) button mushrooms, sliced
8 eggs
2 tablespoons chopped rosemary
1 tablespoon grated Parmesan cheese
1 large round focaccia loaf
sea salt and freshly ground black pepper

1 Put the onion in a frying pan with the oil and slowly fry until softened and golden brown. Add the potatoes, cover the pan and slowly cook for 10–20 minutes (this will depend on the thickness of the potatoes), stirring frequently until the potatoes are golden brown and soft.

2 Add the red and green peppers, courgettes and mushrooms and lightly fry together for 2–3 minutes. Spread the vegetables over the base of the pan.

3 Beat the eggs with the rosemary, salt and pepper. Pour over the vegetables, reduce the heat and cook slowly for 10–20 minutes or until the eggs set.

4 Cover the pan halfway through cooking, and if the top of the frittata remains runny, place the pan under the grill and cook until just set.

5 Loosen the frittata from the pan and turn it out on to a board. While it is still hot, sprinkle the Parmesan over the top and leave to melt. Slice the focaccia in half horizontally and lightly grill. Place the whole frittata between the 2 slices of bread to make a large sandwich. Cut into thick slices and serve warm with salad, or leave until cold and wrap in greaseproof paper for a packed lunch.

Serves 4
Preparation time: 10 minutes
Cooking time: 45 minutes

Cashew Nut and Oriental Vegetable Stir-Fry

1 Heat the oil in a wok or large frying-pan and when very hot add the green and red peppers, red onion, carrots, choi sum and beansprouts. Stir-fry over a high heat for 3–4 minutes or until piping hot.

2 Mix the oyster, hoisin and soy sauce with the water and add to the pan. Stir-fry for a further 1 minute.

3 Add the cashew nuts and sesame seeds and toss together. Add the coriander leaves, and serve immediately with brown rice or egg noodles.

Serves 4–6
Preparation time: 15 minutes
Cooking time: 6 minutes

2 tablespoons vegetable oil
1 green pepper, deseeded and finely sliced
2 red peppers, deseeded and finely sliced
1 red onion, finely sliced
2 carrots, peeled and sliced or cut into strips
125 g (4 oz) choi sum or green cabbage, shredded
175 g (6 oz) beansprouts
2 tablespoons oyster sauce
2 tablespoons hoisin sauce
2–3 tablespoons soy sauce or tamari
5 tablespoons water
75 g (3 oz) cashew nuts, toasted
1 tablespoon sesame seeds, toasted
handful of coriander leaves

Brazil Nut and Sunflower Seed Savoury Cakes

Depending on whether you are counting calories, these little cakes of brazil nuts and chickpeas can be cooked in the oven or fried. Serve with green salad or potato salad with plenty of herbs.

250 g (8 oz) brazil nuts, roughly chopped
2 x 425 g (14 oz) cans organic chickpeas, drained
25 g (1 oz) sunflower seeds
1 tablespoon chopped parsley
1 small onion, finely chopped
2 eggs
125 g (4 oz) wholemeal breadcrumbs
groundnut or vegetable oil, for brushing or
    shallow frying
sea salt and freshly ground black pepper

1 Put the brazil nuts in a blender with the chickpeas. Blend until well mixed and a fairly smooth mixture. Turn the mixture into a bowl, add the sunflower seeds, parsley and onion and mix together until well combined.

2 Beat one of the eggs with salt and pepper, add to the chickpea mixture and blend together well. Take a large tablespoon of the mixture, press into a flat patty and lay on a lightly greased baking sheet. Repeat with the remaining mixture to make 8 large or 16 small patties.

3 Beat the remaining egg, dip each patty into it, then coat in the breadcrumbs. Chill for 4 hours or overnight.

4 Either heat the oil until hot and shallow-fry the cakes for 3–4 minutes on either side or until golden brown, or preheat the oven to 200°C (400°F), Gas Mark 6, brush the nut cakes with a little oil and bake in the preheated oven for 20 minutes, carefully turning once. Serve with steamed vegetables and a tomato sauce or with a mixed green salad and couscous.

Serves 4
Preparation time: 25 minutes, plus chilling
Cooking time: 20 minutes

Grilled Grapefruit, Prawn and Hazelnut Salad

2 large pink grapefruit
75 g (3 oz) hazelnuts or peanuts
pinch of chilli flakes
2 teaspoons honey
pinch of paprika
250 g (8 oz) cooked peeled prawns
75 g (3 oz) beansprouts
1 tablespoon chopped fresh coriander or parsley
1 tablespoon groundnut or olive oil
2 tablespoons lemon juice
sea salt and freshly ground black pepper

1 Cut the grapefruit in half and loosen each segment but leave the flesh in the grapefruit 'shell'.

2 Lightly toast the hazelnuts or peanuts in a hot dry pan, shaking them frequently. Remove from the pan and allow them to cool, then roughly chop.

3 Sprinkle the chilli flakes, 1 teaspoon of the honey and the paprika over the grapefruit flesh and place under the grill for 5–6 minutes until bubbling.

4 Spoon the grapefruit segments out of the shell and add to a bowl with the prawns, beansprouts, coriander or parsley and nuts and toss together.

5 Mix together the remaining honey, the oil, lemon juice, salt, pepper and any grapefruit juice from the shells, pour over the salad and toss.

Serves 4
Preparation time: 15 minutes
Cooking time: 10 minutes

Broccoli and Butter Bean Bake

1 Preheat the oven to 180°C (350°F), Gas Mark 4. Put the onions in a large pan with the oil and fry until golden brown and softened. Add the milk, flour and herbs and slowly bring to the boil, whisking all the time with a balloon whisk.

2 Once the sauce is boiling, reduce the heat and cook for 2–3 minutes or until thickened. Add the tomatoes, salt and pepper and mix well.

3 Add the butter beans, broccoli and parsley to the sauce and bring to the boil, stirring. Pour into a lightly greased 1 litre (1¾ pint) ovenproof dish.

4 Mix the breadcrumbs with the Parmesan or Cheddar and sprinkle over the top. Cook in the centre of the preheated oven for 20–25 minutes or until the breadcrumbs are golden brown and the sauce is bubbling.

5 Serve as a main course with salad or as an accompanying vegetable with grilled chicken, white fish or sausages.

Serves 4–6
Preparation time: 15 minutes
Cooking time: 35 minutes

Beans are an excellent meat substitute and are rich in minerals and fibre.

1 small onion, finely chopped
1 tablespoon vegetable or olive oil
300 ml (½ pint) skimmed milk
2 tablespoons plain or gluten-free flour
½ teaspoon dried mixed herbs
4 tomatoes, peeled, deseeded and chopped
425 g (14 oz) can organic butter beans, drained
150 g (5 oz) small broccoli florets
2 tablespoons chopped parsley
50 g (2 oz) wholemeal breadcrumbs
1 tablespoon grated Parmesan or Cheddar cheese
sea salt and freshly ground black pepper

Lamb Steaks with Italian and Green Beans

Meat is a good source of zinc, iron and some of the B vitamins, but it is best to choose cuts of meat that are lean and therefore lower in saturated fat.

4 x 150 g (5 oz) lean lamb leg steaks
2 onions, chopped
2 tablespoons vegetable or olive oil
2 garlic cloves, crushed
425 g (14 oz) can organic cannellini or butter beans, drained
1 tablespoon molasses
425 g (14 oz) can organic chopped tomatoes
2 tablespoons tomato purée
150 g (5 oz) green beans, trimmed
125 g (4 oz) spinach leaves
sea salt and freshly ground black pepper
coriander leaves, to garnish

1 Season the lamb steaks with salt and pepper. Gently fry the onions in the oil until soft and golden brown. Add the garlic and cook for 1 further minute.

2 Add the drained canned beans to the pan with the molasses, canned tomatoes and tomato purée and bring to a fast simmer.

3 Place the green beans in a steamer over the simmering beans. Reduce the heat slightly, cover the steamer with a lid and cook for 15 minutes. Add a little water to the beans if they begin to dry out.

4 Heat a cast-iron pan or griddle until hot. Lightly oil the lamb steaks and cook for 4–5 minutes on each side for medium-cooked lamb or 6–8 minutes for well cooked.

5 Meanwhile add the spinach leaves to the beans in the tomato sauce. Stir well and season to taste with salt and pepper.

6 Serve the lamb steaks on top of a bed of Italian beans and spinach and top with the steamed green beans. Garnish with coriander.

Serves 4
Preparation time: 20 minutes
Cooking time: 25 minutes

Pumpkin Seed and Muesli Soda Bread

1 Preheat the oven to 200°C (400°F), Gas Mark 6. Grease and flour a 1 kg (2 lb) and a 500 g (1 lb) loaf tin.

2 Sift the flour, cream of tartar and bicarbonate of soda together into a bowl. Add the sugar, raisins, sultanas, chopped nuts and pumpkin or sunflower seeds and mix together well.

3 Add the buttermilk and warm water and mix all the ingredients together into a soft dough. Put the dough into the greased tins and bake in the centre of the preheated oven for 40–45 minutes or until golden brown and cooked through.

4 Remove the loaves from the oven, leave to cool, then turn out on a cooling rack.

5 Serve warm or leave to cool completely. Keep wrapped in greaseproof paper and loosely covered in a large plastic bag. Store in a cool place.

Serves 8–10
Preparation time: 10 minutes
Cooking time: 40 minutes

This loaf is ideal for breakfast or teatime with honey, and great for avocado, tomato and goat's cheese sandwiches. Make double the quantity and keep a loaf ready sliced in the freezer.

500 g (1 lb) gluten-free flour or strong plain bread flour
2 teaspoons cream of tartar
2 teaspoons bicarbonate of soda
2 teaspoons light muscovado sugar
125 g (4 oz) raisins
50 g (2 oz) sultanas
50 g (2 oz) mixed chopped nuts
1 tablespoon pumpkin or sunflower seeds
284 ml (9 fl oz) buttermilk
200 ml (7 fl oz) warm water

Walnut and Sunflower Seed Snacks

Health in a nutshell: walnuts are rich in omega-6 oils and have the added bonus of also being high in omega-3 oils. Like other nuts they are also packed with potassium and vitamin E. Buy nuts as fresh as possible and in their shells if you can, and add a few to a packed lunch. Raw or lightly toasted nuts are best since heat reduces their sensitive essential fats.

4 tablespoons sunflower seeds
25 g (1 oz) sesame seeds
250 g (8 oz) walnut pieces, roughly chopped
1 tablespoon raisins
3 tablespoons set honey

1 Preheat the grill. Mix together the sunflower and sesame seeds, spread over a baking sheet and lightly toast for 2–3 minutes or until the sesame seeds are a light golden colour.

2 Add the walnut pieces and raisins to the toasted seeds and mix together. While the seeds are still warm, mix in the honey. Divide the mixture into walnut-sized portions and, with damp hands, firmly press into 'balls'.

3 Place the balls on baking parchment and either leave as balls or slightly flatten with the heel of the hand. Leave to cool and dry for 3–4 hours or overnight.

4 Store in an airtight container, interleaved with baking parchment.

Makes 24
Preparation time: 10 minutes, plus cooling and drying
Cooking time: 2–3 minutes

Molasses with Muesli and Thick Yogurt

125 g (4 oz) rolled oats
40 g (1½ oz) toasted wheatgerm
40 g (1½ oz) desiccated coconut
50 g (2 oz) sesame seeds
50 g (2 oz) sunflower seeds
25 g (1 oz) pumpkin seeds
1 tablespoon molasses
3 tablespoons clear honey
125 g (4 oz) raisins
75 g (3 oz) sultanas
sliced fresh fruit, such as papaya, banana,
    apple or pineapple
molasses and thick yogurt, to serve

1 Preheat the oven to 190°C (375°F), Gas Mark 5. Put the oats, wheatgerm, coconut, sesame, sunflower and pumpkin seeds in a bowl and mix together.

2 Mix the molasses and honey together and mix into the dry ingredients. Spread the clumps of muesli on a baking sheet and bake in the centre of the preheated oven for 10–15 minutes, stirring frequently to evenly toast the muesli and break up any large lumps.

3 Remove from the oven and leave to cool. Add the raisins and sultanas to the mixture and mix well. Store in an airtight container for 1–2 weeks.

4 Serve the muesli in a deep bowl, with slices of fresh fruit, a large spoonful or two of yogurt and a drizzle of molasses.

Serves 8–10
Preparation time: 10 minutes
Cooking time: 10–15 minutes

Fig and Molasses Cake Bars

1 Preheat the oven to 180°C (350°F), Gas Mark 4. Grease and line an 18 x 28 cm (7 x 11 in) cake tin.

2 Beat the butter, sugar and molasses together until smooth and creamy. Add the beaten eggs slowly, beating well between each addition.

3 Add the hazelnuts, vanilla extract, flour, baking powder and cinnamon and mix thoroughly into the creamed butter.

4 Stir the figs or dates into the mixture and spoon the mixture into the prepared cake tin. Bake in the centre of the preheated oven for 20–25 minutes or until firm to the touch.

5 Remove from the oven and leave to cool slightly before cutting into bars. Turn out of the tin and serve, or leave to cool completely and store in an airtight container for 2–3 days.

Makes 14
Preparation time: 25 minutes
Cooking time: 25 minutes

Molasses is a superfood. It is packed with B vitamins, magnesium, iron, copper and manganese and, per volume, it contains more calcium than milk.

125 g (4 oz) butter
50 g (2 oz) unrefined raw cane caster sugar
3 tablespoons molasses
3 eggs, beaten
50 g (2 oz) hazelnuts, roughly chopped
1 teaspoon vanilla extract
175 g (6 oz) gluten-free or self-raising flour
1 teaspoon baking powder
½ teaspoon ground cinnamon
125 g (4 oz) dried ready-to-eat figs or dates, roughly chopped

Almond Milk Jelly with Mango

If preferred, this milk jelly can be made with soya milk instead of evaporated milk and then sweetened to taste. For vegetarians, use soaked agar agar or agar powder instead of gelatine.

300 ml (½ pint) water
4 tablespoons ground almonds
75 g (3 oz) unrefined raw cane caster sugar
150 ml (¼ pint) sheep's or soya milk
2 sachets gelatine
150 ml (¼ pint) hot but not boiling water
1 teaspoon almond extract
2 mangoes
400 g (13 oz) canned lychees, drained and juice reserved
1 tablespoon toasted flaked almonds
mint sprigs, to garnish

1 Put the water in a pan with the ground almonds and sugar and slowly bring to the boil. Boil for 5–6 minutes, stirring frequently. Add the sheep's or soya milk, return to the boil and remove from the heat.

2 Stir the gelatine into the measured hot but not boiling water and stir briskly until the gelatine has dissolved.

3 Stir this mixture into the almond milk with the almond extract and keep stirring until well combined. Pour the mixture into a square dish or tin and chill for 2–3 hours or until set.

4 When firmly set, use a sharp knife to cut the jelly into diamond or square shapes. Cut the mangoes in half, either side of the central stone. Slice the mango flesh and remove the skin, and serve alongside the almond jelly with the lychees.

5 Sprinkle with toasted almonds and spoon a little reserved lychee juice over the jellies. Garnish with sprigs of mint.

Serves 6
Preparation time: 20 minutes, plus chilling
Cooking time: 6 minutes

Peach and Tofu Smoothie

Tofu is an excellent source of protein and other nutrients. Start each day with a tofu smoothie made with a mix of seasonal or dried fruit. Make the smoothie just before drinking, if possible, although it could be made an hour or so in advance and kept in the refrigerator.

50 g (2 oz) dried ready-to-eat peaches, roughly
    chopped
75 g (3 oz) tofu
300 ml (½ pint) apple juice, chilled
crushed ice or ice cubes (optional)

1 Put the chopped dried peaches in a blender together with the tofu. Add a little of the apple juice and blend the ingredients together to a smooth purée.

2 Add the remainder of the apple juice to the blender and blend together until smooth and frothy.

3 Pour into a tall glass, adding crushed ice or ice cubes if using, and serve with a slice of toasted wholemeal or rye bread for a complete breakfast.

Serves 1–2
Preparation time: 5 minutes

memory boosters

As the body ages, it goes through various changes. Some of these are visible, like greying hair or wrinkled skin, and some are not so apparent. Many people feel that they no longer think as clearly or learn as quickly as they did. The most common complaint is increasing forgetfulness. Although in extreme cases, poor memory may be the result of Alzheimer's disease or dementia, it is becoming clear that many problems with memory may be due to a lack of brain-boosting nutrients in the diet.

Free radicals and antioxidants

Researchers now agree that many of the signs of ageing are the result of free-radical activity. Free radicals are chemicals that attack the body's cells and cause irreparable damage. Basically, they are atoms that have become chemically very active because they have an unpaired electron. Electrons usually revolve around the centre of an atom in pairs. When there is an unpaired electron, the atom attacks other atoms in cells 'looking for another electron'. This can result in a lot of damage to the cells in the body and brain.

Common sources of free radicals are pollution, fried foods, radiation and sunlight. However, the body also produces free radicals when fighting infections, exercising and simply breathing. Over time, free-radical damage accumulates and gradually signs of ageing become more and more apparent. The brain is particularly vulnerable to free-radical damage because these harmful chemicals are attracted to fatty tissues and the brain's structure is primarily fat.

Help is at hand in the form of nutrients called antioxidants, which combat the effects of free radicals. Antioxidants incapacitate free radicals and block their path of destruction. A plentiful supply of antioxidants in the diet can help to slow down the signs of ageing and may boost a failing memory. Luckily, many healthy foods are rich sources of antioxidants.

Antioxidant foods

The key antioxidant vitamins are A, C and E. Found in abundance in fresh fruits and vegetables, these vitamins work together to protect the brain and body by disarming free radicals. In their work as antioxidants, vitamin C and vitamin E work together, to make each other more effective. This is called synergy between nutrients. In fact, vitamin C recycles vitamin E, allowing it to carry on working longer. A diet rich in fruits and vegetables will help to protect the brain and preserve the memory.

In 1999, the American Journal of Epidemiology reported a study investigating the protective effects of antioxidants on memory. More than 5000 men and women aged 60 and older were given memory tests and had blood samples taken from them. The researchers concluded that those with high levels of vitamin E in their blood were found to have the best memories. This research confirms the importance of the role of vitamin E in boosting memory.

Since we know that the antioxidant nutrients work together, it is important to eat lots of antioxidant-rich fruits and vegetables for maximum brain protection and improved recall.

Anthocyanidins

Recently, researchers have discovered some very powerful antioxidants called anthocyanidins – thought to be 50 times more powerful than vitamin E, providing strong protection for the brain from the damaging effects of free radicals.

Found in abundance in certain fruits and berries (in fruits, stems, bark and seeds, flowers and leaves) anthocyanidins are interesting because they can provide protection from a wide variety of toxins and free radicals in both watery and fatty parts of the body. This is in contrast to other antioxidants like vitamin C, which protect only watery parts of the body, while vitamins A and E protect fatty tissues. The significance of this dual role becomes apparent when we consider the composition of the human body – most organs have both fatty and watery components.

Once again, colour can give us a clue as to the relative merits of selected fruits. Red, purple and blue fruits, and in particular berries, are rich in anthocyanidins and will give maximum protection to precious brain cells.

B vitamins make brain energy

The brain consumes almost 25 per cent of the energy used in the body. In order to convert food into energy to power neuromessages, the brain depends on all the B vitamins: B1, B2, B3, B5, B6, folic acid and B12. The elderly seem to be particularly prone to vitamin B12 deficiency. This may be due to inefficient digestion and poor absorption. Without these energy makers, the brain is less alert and thinking slows down. B vitamins are found in brewers' yeast, liver and whole grains such as brown rice and barley.

Tips

One reason the ageing body becomes deficient in vitamins and minerals is that it is less efficient at digesting and absorbing nutrients. Chewing each mouthful of food 20–30 times can aid the body in extracting nutrients.

Drinking 1–2 litres (2–4 pints) of still water each day can increase alertness and awareness.

Stress can inhibit recall at any age. Increasing certain key nutrients, such as vitamins B5 and C, may help to protect against the effects of long-term stress or the stress of a traumatic event (see page 88).

Disorders affecting memory

Presenile dementia is a brain disorder that begins in middle age and results in progressive memory loss, personality changes and deterioration of mental faculties. It is thought to be caused by hardening of the arteries. The clogged arteries slowly reduce the supply of nutrient-rich blood to the brain and, as the brain is starved of these important nutrients, cognitive function starts to suffer. Eventually the person may succumb to a stroke (an interruption of the blood supply to a part of the brain), leading to partial paralysis, coma or death.

A diet rich in the essential fatty acids will encourage healthy blood vessels, reduce blood pressure and lower cholesterol levels. High-fibre foods will also lower cholesterol, and lots of dark leafy green vegetables, nuts, seeds, wheatgerm and whole grains will provide rich sources of vitamin E to improve the body's circulation.

For maximum protection against disorders like dementia avoid sugar, sweets, fried foods, foods high in fat and processed foods. Also avoid caffeine and alcohol. Smoking and lack of exercise are also key risk factors. Exercise increases circulation and helps to deliver important nutrients to the brain.

Alzheimer's disease

Alzheimer's is characterized by symptoms that include depression, distorted perceptions, inability to concentrate and progressive memory loss. It usually strikes after the age of 60 or 65, although it can be found in younger people. Over 4 million people in the United States are currently believed to suffer with Alzheimer's.

Despite extensive research, the precise cause of the disease is not known. It is believed that genes play a role to some extent, but like other degenerative diseases, environmental factors are also likely to have a significant role. Scientists have observed that Alzheimer's sufferers tend to have

---

Memory blocks

- ☐ Excessive consumption of alcohol will interfere with vitamins A, D, E, K, all the B vitamins, and magnesium. This can lead to fuzzy thinking and poor recall.
- ☐ Coffee, tea, and soft drinks containing caffeine can upset the delicate blood sugar balance, which can lead to poor concentration, reduced alertness and forgetfulness.

low levels of B vitamins and zinc, both of which are important in cognitive functioning. Processed foods tend to contain little of these key brain boosters.

Some studies have reported an association between aluminium and Alzheimer's, and high levels of aluminium have been found in the brains of some Alzheimer's patients. This has led experts to recommend that aluminium cookware should be avoided, especially when cooking acidic foods. Stainless steel, glass and iron cookware are widely available alternatives.

Antioxidant-rich foods are particularly important for protecting brain cells from free-radical damage, as is avoiding exposure to free radicals in the first place. Eating whole, unprocessed and unrefined foods may reduce the risk of Alzheimer's disease and will certainly boost the natural protection of the brain and nerve cells.

Foods in focus

Antioxidant foods can delay the effects of ageing on mental performance. Key antioxidant vitamins A and E protect the fatty parts of the brain and body, including the nerve cell membranes. Vitamin C works with vitamin E for maximum antioxidant power.

Berries

New research has declared berries to be the anti-ageing food of the 21st century. The active ingredient is a group of flavonoids called anthocyanidins (see page 67), which are powerful antioxidants. Anthocyanidins have also been found to prevent collagen from breaking down. Collagen is the elastic component in skin, joints and, in particular, veins and arteries, which carry nutrients to the brain. Anthocyanidin-rich fruits include blackberries, blueberries, cranberries, black grapes and blackcurrants.

Anthocyanidins are robust nutrients and survive various food processes, so when fresh berries are not available, canned and frozen berries are nutritious alternatives. In addition to being rich in anthocyanidins, berries boast high levels of vitamin C and beta-carotene (the precursor of vitamin A), which are other key antioxidants.

Carrots and sweet potatoes

The rich orange colour of sweet potatoes and carrots indicate that they are loaded with beta-carotene. This carotenoid pigment converts to vitamin A in the body when needed and is a powerful force in the fight against free radicals. Carrots contain more beta-carotene than any other vegetable. Sweet potatoes are also full of brain-protecting anti-oxidants; in addition to beta-carotene, they are rich in vitamins C and E. Choose the darkest orange specimens for the highest amounts of beta-carotene. Avoid older vegetables which may appear dry and shrivelled with sunken areas around the ends. Beta-carotene is more absorbable when cooked, so bake, steam or boil these delicious root vegetables.

Watercress and peas

Watercress is an excellent source of vitamin C. A mere 100 g (3½ oz) of watercress contains the recommended dietary allowance (RDA) of vitamin C. However, vitamin C is particularly vulnerable to degradation, and as much as 50 per cent can be lost during storage in just two weeks. Always try to buy it fresh and eat as soon as possible after purchase.

Peas are wonderful antioxidants because in addition to providing beta-carotene and vitamin C, they contain more protein than most other vegetables. Pea protein is deficient in the amino acids methionine and cysteine, but these are supplied in ample amounts by cereal grains including rice and wheat. In addition, the legume protein contains sufficient lysine to cover the deficiencies of this amino acid in grain proteins. So a meal that combines peas with a grain has a higher quality of protein than either food alone. These amino acids supply the brain with the basic building blocks of neurotransmitters.

Peas can be bought fresh, frozen, canned and dried. Cooked dried peas provide about twice as much carbohydrates and proteins as cooked fresh peas, however fresh peas are a much better source of the antioxidant vitamins beta-carotene and vitamin C. As a general rule, fresh peas provide more vitamins and minerals than frozen or canned. However, bear in mind that if they are stored for too long they lose much of their nutritional content.

Oily fish

The omega-3 oils found in certain fish are crucial for protecting the parts of our brain that send messages to the body. Fishy sources of these essential fatty acids include mackerel, sardines and kippers. Fresh salmon and tuna also contain high levels of omega-3 oils, although the canned versions of these fish are poorer sources of these vital fats. A diet rich in these fatty acids will not only protect the function of the nervous system, but will also enhance your mental abilities.

Brewers' yeast

Brewers' yeast is a non-leavening yeast that is rich in virtually all the important brain-boosting nutrients. It contains 16 amino acids, 14 minerals and 17 vitamins. It is an excellent memory booster which can provide a tasty addition to many meals. It is usually sold in the form of a powder for use in cooking or as tablets or capsules. Brewers' yeast is rich in the B complex vitamins that provide the co-factors needed to convert food to thinking fuel and to convert amino acids to neurotransmitters. Just 2 tablespoons supplies 86 per cent of the RDA for vitamin B1 and 56 per cent of the RDA for vitamin B3. Rich in iron, chromium, potassium and magnesium, brewers' yeast also supplies the key minerals needed for alertness and concentration.

Caution: Brewers' yeast is high in purines and should be avoided by those with gout or kidney stones. Purines are nitrogen-containing chemicals found in many foods and are excreted from the body as uric acid.

memory booster menu

breakfast
Mid-morning Break 'n' Shake
(*see page 73*)

lunch
. Thick Carrot Soup with Orange and
Ginger (*see page 74*)
Kipper and Brown Rice Kedgeree
(*see page 72*)
small mixed salad

dinner
Spiced Mackerel with Celeriac Mash
(*see page 79*)
steamed peas and carrots
Poached Cherries with Almond Milk
Pudding (*see page 80*)

snacks
fresh fruit
herbal and fruit teas

Kipper and Brown Rice Kedgeree

1 Cook the brown rice in boiling water for 30–35 minutes or until the grains are soft and tender. Drain the rice well.

2 Gently cook the onions in the oil until golden brown and crisp, then add the curry powder and stir for 1–2 minutes.

3 Remove the kipper or mackerel flesh from the skin and bones, and flake into large pieces.

4 Add the flaked fish to the hot onion and curry mixture and toss together over the heat until the fish is hot, taking care to not break the fish up too much.

5 Mix the cooked rice into the fish mixture with the chopped hard-boiled eggs, parsley, dill and sultanas and toss together. Season to taste with salt and pepper. Garnish with dill and serve with mango chutney.

Serves 4–6
Preparation time: 15 minutes
Cooking time: 35 minutes

Kedgeree is a traditional breakfast/ brunch dish, all too often laced with melted butter and cream. This is a far more wholesome version, lightly spiced with a pinch of curry powder and made with energy-sustaining brown rice.

250 g (8 oz) brown basmati rice
2 onions, sliced
3 tablespoons vegetable oil
1 teaspoon curry powder
300 g (10 oz) kippers or smoked mackerel
4 eggs, hard-boiled and chopped
2 tablespoons chopped parsley
1 tablespoon chopped dill
2 tablespoons sultanas
sea salt and freshly ground black pepper
dill, to garnish

Mid-Morning Break 'n' Shake

Make this 'meal-and-a-half in a glass' and drink it mid-morning. Brewers' yeast is a cocktail of B vitamins, minerals and 16 amino acids and is high in phosphorus. It can be added to soups, stews and muesli to provide a large helping of many of the daily essential vitamins. The powdered form has a mild flavour, which blends well with molasses and linseeds.

1 tablespoon brewers' yeast powder
300 ml (½ pint) tropical fruit or apple juice
1 teaspoon molasses
1 teaspoon linseeds

1 Put the brewers' yeast in a blender with the fruit juice and molasses and blend well.

2 Roughly grind the linseeds using a pestle and mortar or add to a small bowl and crush with the end of a rolling-pin. Add to the fruit juice and blend together for 1 minute.

3 Pour the shake into a tall tumbler and drink immediately.

Serves 1
Preparation time: 5 minutes

Thick Carrot Soup with Orange and Ginger

Carrots team well with the other excellent immune-building ingredients of garlic and ginger. Fresh orange juice provides extra antioxidant content.

750 g (1½ lb) carrots, peeled and roughly chopped
5cm (2 in) piece of fresh root ginger, finely chopped
900 ml (1½ pints) vegetable stock or water
2 tablespoons chopped parsley
150 ml (¼ pint) orange juice
sea salt and freshly ground black pepper
buttermilk or thick yogurt, to serve

1 Put the carrots in a pan with the ginger and vegetable stock or water and bring to the boil. Reduce the heat and simmer for 12–15 minutes or until soft and cooked through.

2 Remove from the heat and, working in batches, put the soup in a blender with the parsley, orange juice, salt and pepper and blend until smooth.

3 Return the soup to the pan and adjust the seasoning to taste. Either simmer gently until hot and serve with a little buttermilk or yogurt swirled on top, or serve lukewarm or cold.

Serves 6
Preparation time: 20 minutes
Cooking time: 15 minutes

Pea, Mint and Barley Risotto

Risotto is more usually made with arborio rice but this recipe introduces another grain – pearl barley. It makes a rustic and very wholesome dish, delicious with fresh or frozen peas and plenty of chopped mint.

1 onion, finely chopped

2 garlic cloves, crushed

3 tablespoons olive oil

250 g (8 oz) pearl barley

900 ml (1½ pints) vegetable stock or water

175 g (6 oz) peas

2 tablespoons chopped or torn mint

4 tablespoons grated Parmesan cheese

sea salt and freshly ground black pepper

To serve

grated Parmesan cheese

extra virgin olive oil

1 Put the onion and garlic in a pan with the olive oil and cook gently until soft and beginning to brown. Do not cook over a high heat or the garlic will burn and turn bitter.

2 Add the pearl barley and coat in the oil. Add the vegetable stock or water and bring to the boil. Reduce the heat, cover the pan and simmer for 20 minutes.

3 Add the peas to the pan with black pepper and stir together. Add extra water if the barley is drying out. Cover the pan and simmer the risotto for a further 10 minutes or until the barley is soft and tender.

4 Season to taste and add the mint and Parmesan. Remove from the heat and leave to stand, with a lid on the pan, for 5 minutes. Serve with extra Parmesan and olive oil and a salad of bright green leaves.

Serves 4
Preparation time: 10 minutes
Cooking time: 40 minutes

Sweet Potato and Spinach Mash with Grilled Cod

Sweet potatoes are full of vitamins C, E and A and zinc. Choose darker-coloured ones for the highest amount of these antioxidants.

1kg (2 lb) sweet potatoes, peeled and roughly cubed
175 g (6 oz) baby spinach leaves, torn
2 tablespoons extra virgin olive oil
1 tablespoon crushed mixed peppercorns
4 x 150 g (5 oz) thick cod fillets
sea salt and freshly ground black pepper
lemon or lime wedges, to serve

1 Steam the sweet potato cubes in a steamer over boiling water for 10–15 minutes or until just soft. Remove while hot, put into a bowl and roughly mash.

2 Add the torn spinach leaves, salt, pepper and olive oil and mix together. If the sweet potato is still hot the spinach leaves will wilt into the mash. Cover and keep warm.

3 Meanwhile, mix some sea salt with the crushed peppercorns and sprinkle over one side of the cod fillets.

4 Preheat the grill and cook the fish, pepper side up, for 8–10 minutes without turning, or until cooked through. Serve the cod on a bed of mashed sweet potato with wedges of lemon or lime.

Serves 4
Preparation time: 15 minutes
Cooking time: 15 minutes

Watercress and Couscous Cannelloni

Watercress contains all the antioxidant vitamins and zinc. It also contains iron and boosts energy.

2 onions, finely chopped
6 tablespoons olive oil
75 g (3 oz) couscous
50 g (2 oz) watercress, finely chopped
12 no-precook cannelloni tubes or sheets of
    fresh lasagne
2 garlic cloves, crushed
1 red chilli, deseeded and finely chopped
    (optional)
2 x 425 g (14 oz) cans organic chopped tomatoes
1 red pepper, deseeded and finely chopped
1 orange pepper, deseeded and finely chopped
2 tablespoons chopped basil or parsley
4 tablespoons grated Parmesan cheese
sea salt and freshly ground black pepper

1 Preheat the oven to 190°C (375°F), Gas Mark 5. Gently cook one of the onions in 2 tablespoons of the olive oil until soft and beginning to brown.

2 Put the couscous in a bowl and cover with boiling water. Leave for 3–4 minutes and then fluff up the grains using a fork. Season well with salt and pepper and stir in the fried onion and the watercress.

3 Using a teaspoon, fill the cannelloni tubes with the couscous and lay them in a lightly greased ovenproof dish. If using lasagne sheets, roll them into tubes, dampen the underside and press the sheets together or carefully secure with cocktail sticks. Fill as before.

4 Meanwhile, heat the remaining oil and slowly cook the remaining onion with the garlic until soft. Add the chilli, if using, and the canned tomatoes and peppers, and bring to a fast simmer. Simmer, covered, for 10 minutes.

5 Season the sauce with salt and pepper, add the chopped basil or parsley and pour evenly over the pasta tubes. Sprinkle the Parmesan over the dish and cook in the centre of the preheated oven for 20–25 minutes or until the pasta is cooked. Serve with a crisp green salad, removing cocktail sticks before eating.

Serves 4–6
Preparation time: 30 minutes
Cooking time: 35 minutes

Sardines with Spinach Pesto and Roasted Pumpkin

Sardines can be grilled quickly but when there are a lot to cook it can be easier to roast them. They are served here with roasted pumpkin and a strong and vibrant spinach pesto packed with iron.

500 g (1 lb) pumpkin or squash
2 tablespoons vegetable or olive oil
2 red onions, cut into thick wedges
16 sardines, gutted and descaled
1–2 garlic cloves, crushed
12 tablespoons extra virgin olive oil
75 g (3 oz) young spinach leaves
50 g (2 oz) walnuts, roughly chopped
1 tablespoon grated Parmesan cheese
sea salt and freshly ground black pepper
lemon wedges, to serve

1 Preheat the oven to 220°C (425°F), Gas Mark 7. Cut the pumpkin into large chunks, cut away the skin, and scoop out the seeds.

2 Put the vegetable or olive oil in a large roasting tin. Add the pumpkin and red onion wedges and toss in the oil. Roast in the centre of the preheated oven for 35 minutes, turning often, until soft and charred in places.

3 While the vegetables are cooking put the prepared sardines on a baking sheet. Season well with salt and pepper and cook at the top of the oven for 10–15 minutes or until cooked through.

4 Put the garlic cloves in a blender with half the extra virgin olive oil and blend for a minute. Add the spinach, walnuts, salt and pepper and blend together to a rough purée. Add the Parmesan and remaining olive oil and blend together.

5 Serve the cooked sardines on a bed of roasted vegetables and spoon the spinach pesto over the top. Add wedges of lemon and serve.

Serves 4
Preparation time: 25 minutes
Cooking time: 35 minutes

Spiced Mackerel with Celeriac Mash

1 Mix the cumin seeds, peppercorns and chilli flakes together. Put the mackerel into a shallow container, sprinkle the spices over the fish and coat evenly in the mixture. Cover the dish and refrigerate for a couple of hours.

2 Preheat the oven to 200°C (400°F), Gas Mark 6. Put the mackerel into an ovenproof dish, stuff the fish with sprigs of dill and pour the cider over and around the fish. Loosely cover the dish with foil and bake in the preheated oven for 15–20 minutes or until the fish are just cooked.

3 Meanwhile put the celeriac into a pan of boiling water and boil for 5 minutes. Add the potatoes and cook together for a further 15–20 minutes or until both the potatoes and celeriac are soft when prodded with the tip of a knife.

4 Drain well and mash the vegetables with the milk and olive oil. Season to taste with salt and pepper. Serve the fish with the potato and celeriac mash and thick wedges of lemon.

Serves 4
Preparation time: 15 minutes, plus marinating
Cooking time: 25 minutes

Mackerel is a delicious and robust fish and contains plenty of the essential fatty acid omega-3.

1 teaspoon cumin seeds
1 teaspoon crushed black peppercorns
pinch of chilli flakes
4 large mackerel, gutted and descaled
handful of dill sprigs
150 ml (¼ pint) dry cider
375 g (12 oz) celeriac, peeled and cubed
750 g (1½ lb) King Edward potatoes, cubed
2 tablespoons milk or soya milk
1–2 tablespoons olive oil
sea salt and freshly ground black pepper
lemon wedges, to serve

Poached Cherries with Almond Milk Pudding

1 Put the cherries, caster sugar and apple juice in a pan and heat very gently for 6–8 minutes, stirring occasionally. Remove from the heat and let cool.

2 Put the milk in a separate pan with the muscovado sugar and bring gently to a fast simmer. Mix the cornflour and ground rice with a little water to a smooth paste and add to the hot milk stirring constantly. Return the milk to the boil, reduce the heat and, still stirring constantly, simmer gently for 5 minutes.

3 Add the almonds to the milk and simmer for a further 10 minutes. Remove from the heat and stir in the almond extract.

4 Allow the almond pudding to cool and serve warm or cold with the poached cherries on top and sprinkled with toasted hazelnuts.

Serves 4–6
Preparation time: 10 minutes
Cooking time: 25 minutes

Mind the cherry stones in this recipe – stone the fruit first if preferred.

500 g (1 lb) black cherries
1 tablespoon unrefined raw cane caster sugar
150 ml (¼ pint) unsweetened apple juice
600 ml (1 pint) milk
1 tablespoon light muscovado sugar
1 tablespoon cornflour
2 tablespoons ground rice
50 g (2 oz) toasted hazelnuts or blanched
   almonds, finely chopped
1 teaspoon almond extract
1 tablespoon crushed toasted hazelnuts

Black Grape Jelly with Citrus Fruit

Black grapes are a great stress-buster, and their juice makes a delicious non-alcoholic drink at any time of the year. Add any of the seasonal berries to this refreshing jelly, and if you are strictly vegetarian opt for agar agar instead of gelatine.

600 ml (1 pint) black grape juice
2 sachets gelatine
175 g (6 oz) seedless red and green grapes, rinsed and halved
1 orange
1 pink grapefruit
1 tablespoon unrefined raw cane caster sugar

1 Put 150 ml (¼ pint) of the grape juice in a small bowl and add the gelatine. Stand the bowl in a pan of simmering water and heat until the gelatine has dissolved. Remove from the heat and allow to cool a little. Add the dissolved gelatine to the remainder of the grape juice and mix together well.

2 Place the grapes in the bottom of 4 tall glasses. Pour in enough of the black grape jelly to just cover the grapes and put the glasses in the refrigerator.

3 Once the jelly in the glasses has set, top up with the remaining jelly (reheat this remaining jelly over hot water if it has also begun to set). Return the glasses to the refrigerator for 2–3 hours to set completely. This two-step setting is not important if you do not mind the grapes floating to the surface of the jelly.

4 Segment the orange and grapefruit, collecting any juice in a small pan. Add the caster sugar to the pan and gently heat until the sugar has dissolved. Bring to a gentle simmer, then remove from the heat, add the orange and grapefruit segments and leave to cool.

5 When the citrus fruits are cold, spoon the segments and a little of the juice on top of the jelly and serve.

Serves 4
Preparation time: 20 minutes, plus chilling
Cooking time: 10 minutes

Blueberry and Blackberry Yogurt Syllabub

1 Put the blackberries in a pan and heat very gently for 2–3 minutes until the juice begins to run out. Remove from the heat and stir in the blueberries.

2 Lightly whisk the cream with the honey, to taste, until softly peaking and then stir in the orange liqueur, if using. Fold the yogurt into the cream.

3 Divide the berries and their juice between 4 dessert glasses or bowls and then top with the yogurt mixture. Sprinkle the top with the flaked almonds and refrigerate for 1–2 hours before serving.

Serves 4
Preparation time: 10 minutes
Cooking time: 2–3 minutes, plus chilling

Blueberries and blackberries work well together and are full of immune-boosting properties.

125 g (4 oz) blackberries
125 g (4 oz) blueberries
150 ml (¼ pint) whipping cream
1–2 tablespoons clear honey
1 tablespoon orange liqueur (optional)
300 ml (½ pint) thick yogurt
1 tablespoon flaked almonds, toasted

Cranberry Compote with Lemon Cake

Cranberries can be used in many savoury or dessert recipes. This compote of cranberries could equally be served with grilled or roast pork or chicken.

175 g (6 oz) cranberries
150 ml (¼ pint) orange or apple juice
4–5 tablespoons honey
thick yogurt or low-fat crème fraîche, to serve
mint sprig, to garnish

Lemon cake
175 g (6 oz) butter
175 g (6 oz) unrefined raw cane caster sugar
3 eggs, beaten
175 g (6 oz) rice flour or plain flour
2 teaspoons baking powder
grated rind and juice of 2 lemons
50 g (2 oz) unrefined raw cane granulated sugar

1 Put the berries in a saucepan with the fruit juice and poach very gently for 10 minutes. Remove from the heat and sweeten with the honey. Leave to cool.

2 Preheat the oven to 200°C (400°F), Gas Mark 6. Grease and line a 20 cm/8 in cake tin. Cream the butter and caster sugar together until fluffy and light. Add the eggs, a little at a time, beating well between each addition. Sift the flour and baking powder together and fold into the creamed mixture with the grated lemon rind. Combine well.

3 Spoon the mixture into the prepared tin, level the surface and bake in the centre of the preheated oven for 35 minutes.

4 Meanwhile, place the lemon juice in a pan with half the granulated sugar and heat gently until the sugar has dissolved. Bring the syrup to the boil. Remove from the heat and leave to cool.

5 Remove the cake from the oven, leave to cool in the tin for 10 minutes and then turn out. Lightly prick the surface of the cake and pour the lemon syrup over the top. Sprinkle with the remaining sugar and let stand for 30 minutes.

6 Serve the cake cut in thick slices, with a large spoonful of cranberry compote and either yogurt or low-fat crème fraîche, and a sprig of mint to decorate.

Serves 6–8
Preparation time: 20 minutes
Cooking time: 45 minutes, plus cooling

stress busters

Stress is sometimes considered a modern everyday illness, but in fact the stress reaction has been fundamental to man's survival through the ages. In prehistoric times, the 'fight-or-flight' reaction helped people to survive life-threatening situations. Today's stresses are of a different nature and what was once a useful reaction can exert excessive demands on the body's nutritional status – eating the right nutrients can help to reduce these demands.

The stress reaction

Under stress, the adrenal glands, which are situated above the kidneys, release a hormone called adrenaline (epinephrine). This kickstarts a variety of physical reactions designed to help the body deal with the crisis. First, the liver releases sugar into the blood to supply a surge of energy so that the body can prepare to fight or flee. Breathing becomes faster so as to take in more oxygen. The heart rate speeds up, pumping the blood faster to carry the extra sugar and oxygen to the brain and muscles. Cholesterol levels rise to thicken the blood so it will clot more easily in the event of injury. Finally, digestion slows down because it is not essential during a crisis.

The stress reaction originally evolved to prepare us for an immediate danger. It enabled prehistoric man to tackle a sabre-toothed tiger to the best of his ability. However, in the 21st century, we are less likely to be presented with the risk of immediate injury or death. Today's stresses are of a different nature and tend to be longer lasting. According to

psychologists, the list of top ten stressful events include serious illness, death and divorce. However, the body also reacts to less serious but often longer-term stresses including financial worries, work deadlines, crowds, noise and traffic jams. Even changes in temperature and toxins in the environment can put extra strains on the body. Although the human body now responds to 21st century stresses, it still reacts as it did for prehistoric man – the effects on the blood supply, breathing and digestion are the same.

Now stress is not altogether a bad thing. It can provide zest and motivation to everyday activities; in small doses it can tone up the body's reaction times and add a bit of excitement to life. But if stress is extreme or long lasting, then the body's reactions can be overwhelming and usually end up being harmful overall. Prolonged stress places tremendous pressure on many vital organs including the heart, blood vessels, adrenal glands and the immune system.

Combating the symptoms of stress

The increased production of adrenaline (epinephrine) responsible for most stress-related symptoms is also the reason for nutritional deficiencies. Hence, the body needs more nutrients to mount a stress reaction.

Many people handle stress very well, but others may succumb to fatigue, insomnia, back and neck aches and high blood pressure. Long-term stress can lead to more frequent colds and flus plus various digestive problems. Since digestion takes a back seat during stress, many people suffer indigestion, heartburn, diarrhoea and constipation. In extreme cases, some people may develop ulcers.

It is estimated that stress may be partially to blame for 80 per cent of illnesses and can be connected to asthma, angina and premenstrual tension syndrome.

Tips

When under stress:

Eat lots of fruit and vegetables to redress the imbalance between potassium and sodium needed for the transmission of nerve messages

Eat in a relaxed environment to ensure complete digestion of important stress-busting vitamins and minerals

Avoid junk foods. These use up valuable nutrients to digest empty calories, cause imbalances in blood sugar levels and can result in symptoms of depression, anxiety and irritability

Avoid foods that may cause an allergic reaction. These can lead to a stress reaction

Reduce your caffeine intake. Drink herbal and fruit teas instead

Do not drink alcohol, smoke tobacco or take recreational drugs

Exercise is often found to help in dealing with stress. Yoga can be extremely beneficial as you will learn meditation and deep-breathing exercises – both useful stress-relievers. Late nights and a hectic lifestyle make life more stressful, so a regular sleep pattern will also help to reduce levels of stress.

Anti-stress nutrition

When the body is under stress, it needs certain nutrients in abundance. The B vitamins are important for converting protein, carbohydrates and fats into energy in order to fulfil the increased needs during a stress reaction. Vitamin B5, which is essential for adrenal function, is considered the 'anti-stress vitamin' because it helps the body cope with stress.

The antioxidants, vitamins A, C and E, are needed to fight the free radicals, which are the natural byproducts of stress. In addition, vitamin C is a key vitamin for the adrenal glands and is easily depleted when the adrenal glands are working overtime.

It is not only vitamins that are required when the body is in stress, certain minerals are also important anti-stress nutrients. Extra potassium is needed because the increased energy production causes potassium to be excreted, and potassium plays a role in nerve cell function. Magnesium is needed for efficient nerve transmission – when depleted during stress, a deficiency can result in fatigue, mental confusion, irritability and insomnia. Lastly, calcium

is required for healthy nerves and works with magnesium to reduce irritability and insomnia.

Under stress the body can use up many of the key nutrients needed for the efficient functioning of the nervous system. To add insult to injury, the body digests and absorbs food less efficiently, so it is not capable of replacing the key stress vitamins and minerals. Thus prolonged stress can lead to nutrient deficiencies, which in turn exacerbate the symptoms of stress. A vicious circle develops.

Our ability to cope with stress naturally is also compounded by certain substances. It is tempting, when under stress, to turn to comforts such as chocolates, alcohol or smoking. However, tobacco and alcohol, and some recreational drugs, compound the chemical stresses, increase adrenal output and interfere with the normal brain chemistry. They can also interfere with sleep patterns. Contrary to popular belief, studies show that alcohol can significantly increase feelings of anxiety. In 1999, the *American Journal of Psychiatry* reported the results of a study among college students on the link between alcohol and stress. It found that the odds of developing an anxiety disorder were four times greater in students with an alcohol dependency than in those without.

Similarly, caffeine has been shown to have an association with stress. In some people it can induce irritability, anxiety, panic attacks, depression and insomnia.

Symptoms of stress include:

- ☐ Fatigue
- ☐ Insomnia
- ☐ Back and neck ache
- ☐ Headaches
- ☐ Dizziness
- ☐ Tearfulness
- ☐ High blood pressure
- ☐ Frequent colds and flus
- ☐ Digestive problems: indigestion, heartburn, diarrhoea, constipation, even ulcers

Key anti-stress nutrients

B vitamins
- ☐ support the nervous system
- ☐ improve concentration and memory
- ☐ ease depression
- ☐ relieve irritability
- ☐ are important for extra energy production under the influence of adrenaline
- ☐ are found in liver and brewers' yeast

Vitamin B5 (the 'anti-stress vitamin')
- ☐ improves coping mechanism
- ☐ supports adrenal glands
- ☐ helps reduce allergic reactions (which in themselves can stress the body)
- ☐ is found in mushrooms and avocado

Vitamin C
- ☐ is essential for healthy adrenal glands
- ☐ a deficiency can lead to irritability
- ☐ is a key antioxidant to fight free radicals, the by-products of stress
- ☐ is found in blackcurrants, green pepper, mango and papaya

Iron
- ☐ carries oxygen to the brain
- ☐ is found in liver, wholemeal bread, eggs and meat

Magnesium
- ☐ is essential for nerve function
- ☐ a deficiency can result in a predisposition to stress, irritability, insomnia, fatigue and mental confusion
- ☐ is found in green leafy vegetables

Calcium
- ☐ is essential for nerve function
- ☐ has a calming, tranquillizing effect
- ☐ relieves insomnia
- ☐ reduces irritability
- ☐ is found in dairy products as well as green leafy vegetables

Anxiety and panic attacks

Many people suffer from anxiety or panic attacks. It is thought that in some cases these may be due to a sudden drop in blood sugar levels. Low blood sugar may be a reaction to foods that originally caused a sugar surge. The body finds the sugar level uncomfortably high and the attempt to reduce this causes hypoglycaemia (low blood sugar). This can lead to a rapid heart beat, fast, shallow breathing, dizziness and feelings of panic.

In a 1981 edition of *Biological Psychiatry* researchers suggested that people who get panic attacks may be suffering from a lack of the essential fatty acid omega-3, the fatty acid found in oily fish, including mackerel and sardines. In the study, 75 per cent of subjects with a long history of panic attacks improved within two months after increasing their omega-3 intake. Other signs of essential fatty acid deficiency are dandruff, dry skin and brittle nails.

Foods in focus

Eating foods rich in the anti-stress nutrients is a good way of helping your body cope naturally with the effects of ongoing stress.

Avocado

Avocados are much maligned in some quarters because of their high fat content. However most of the fat in this fruit is the monounsaturated variety and thus is easily digested and has none of the artery-clogging effects of saturated fat. Avocados are rich in antioxidant vitamins A, C and E, which will protect brain cells from the free radical damage induced by high stress levels. They are also good sources of important adrenal-supporting B vitamins; one avocado will supply one-third of the recommended dietary allowance (RDA) for anti-stress vitamin B5. They are also rich in potassium, which is needed to ward off mental confusion and depression. Most avocados reach supermarkets in an

unripened form. As the avocado ripens it also starts to lose the important antioxidant nutrients, especially vitamin C. Because of this, avocados should be eaten as soon as they are ripe and not stored for too long.

Mushrooms

Mushrooms are high in water content and low in calories. They contain 20 per cent more protein than potatoes (weight for weight) and are packed with adrenal-supporting B vitamins, particularly vitamin B5.

Best-quality young mushrooms look fresh and have closed caps. Mushrooms with caps that are partially open and brown or black 'gills' (the fluted formation between cap and stem) are older specimens. Both fresh and dried mushrooms are rich in the phytochemicals required to protect against the stress reaction.

Shiitake and reishi mushrooms contain the phytochemical lentinan, a powerful immune stimulant. These mushrooms are particularly popular in Japan where claims have been made that they have qualities to prevent and treat cancer, as well as high blood cholesterol, high blood pressure, viral diseases and sticky blood platelets.

Spring greens and spinach

Leafy green vegetables are rich sources of the synergistic minerals calcium and magnesium, which work together to ensure efficient nerve transmissions. Calcium is a natural tranquillizer, which helps to soothe irritability and aids insomnia. Half a cup of cooked spinach contains more calcium, magnesium and iron than half a cup of milk, so these can really be considered essential foods. Cooking can reduce these key minerals, so ensure they are cooked lightly. Leafy greens are particularly rich in antioxidants, with beta-carotene giving spinach its very dark green colour.

When buying spinach, look for clean, fresh, dark green leaves. Yellow, discoloured and crushed leaves should be avoided because they will probably have lost some of the nutritional value. Eat as fresh as possible to get the most vitamin C from greens. *Caution*: Spinach contains oxalic acid, which can interfere with the absorption of calcium by preventing it from dissolving into a usable form. When served with calcium-rich dairy products the goodness of the dairy products is diminished, so avoid this combination in order to benefit fully from the nutrients.

Liver

Organ meats tend to be very rich sources of protein and the B vitamins. Liver, in particular, is chock full of nutrients to help with stress. Compared with muscle meat, liver has at least double the levels of most B vitamins, and ten times the amount of vitamin B5, the anti-stress vitamin. An average 175 g (6 oz) serving of sautéed lamb's liver will provide the RDA for vitamins B2, B3, B5, B12 and folic acid. The liver usually contains almost four times the amount of iron found in muscle meat. The B vitamins replace nutrients used in the stress reaction and provide energy for the brain, while iron is vital for mental alertness. Lamb's liver is nutritionally superior to both chicken and calves' liver.

Because one of the liver's roles in both humans and animals is to handle toxins and waste products, it is best to choose the livers of young animals for eating – and preferably from an organic source. This way you can be sure that it is free from the cocktail of chemicals with which most meats are laced. The hormones, growth accelerators and accumulated residue of pesticides in the meat we consume may well interfere with the normal production of neurotransmitters in our brains.

Millet

Millet has been grown in Asia and North Africa since prehistoric times and is a staple part of the diet of millions of people. It is about 70 per cent starch and converts in the body to glucose to make energy for the brain. It also contains more and better-quality protein than wheat, rice or corn, making millet a good builder of neurotransmitters. Millet is now finding its way into many US and European health food stores in the form of flour and flakes, and in pasta and breakfast cereals.

Guava and papaya

Under stress, the body and brain require lots of vitamin C. The tropical fruits guava and papaya are the richest fruit sources of this vitamin. Vitamin C is also a potent antioxidant to fight the free radicals caused by stress, which can harm fragile brain and nervous cells. One guava has three times more vitamin C than an orange, while one papaya has more than double the vitamin C.

Vitamin C reduces with each day of storage, so look for unblemished fresh fruits and eat as soon as possible after purchase.

Papaya also contains papain, a beneficial enzyme which helps with protein digestion.

stress-busting menu

Breakfast
Molasses with muesli and thick yogurt
unsweetened fruit juice

Lunch
Mango and Avocado Salad with
   Smoked Chicken (*see page 97*)
mushroom soup
Walnut and Sunflower Seed Snacks
   (*see page 59*)

Dinner
Griddled Liver and Bacon with Grilled
   Potatoes (*see page 94*)
steamed spinach
Poached Guava with Yogurt Brûlée
   (*see page 101*)

Snacks
fresh fruit, especially papaya
herbal and fruit teas

Griddled Liver and Bacon with Grilled Potatoes

The trick with iron-rich liver is to not overcook it and to serve it with plenty of flavoursome gravy.

500 g (1 lb) salad or Charlotte potatoes
4 tablespoons olive oil
leaves from 1 rosemary sprig
2 large onions, 1 thinly sliced, 1 thickly sliced
2 teaspoons light muscovado sugar or molasses
450 ml (¾ pint) vegetable or lamb stock
1 tablespoon cornflour, mixed to a smooth paste
    with a little water
6 streaky bacon rashers
600 g (1¼ lb) lamb's liver, trimmed, thickly sliced
    and seasoned with salt and pepper
sea salt and freshly ground black pepper

1 Boil the potatoes for 6–8 minutes until just tender. Drain, refresh under cold water and halve. Mix with 3 tablespoons of olive oil and the rosemary.

2 Fry the thinly sliced onion in the remaining oil until golden brown. Add the sugar or molasses and stir until the onion is caramelized. Add the stock and bring to the boil. Reduce the heat, cover and simmer gently for 10 minutes.

3 Stir the cornflour paste into the gravy. Bring it slowly to the boil, stirring constantly until thickened. Season to taste. Place the potatoes on a baking sheet and grill for 8–10 minutes, turning frequently until golden brown.

4 Heat a griddle or large frying-pan until hot. Add the bacon and thickly sliced onion and cook over a medium heat for 6 minutes, turning once. Remove and keep warm. Add the liver to the pan and cook for 3–4 minutes on each side.

5 Serve the liver on a pile of grilled potatoes. Top with the griddled onions and bacon and pour the hot onion gravy over and around.

Serves 4
Preparation time: 15 minutes
Cooking time: 35 minutes

Mushrooms with Millet Spaghetti

Full of flavour and texture, mushrooms are an ideal alternative to meat in terms of both taste and nutrient levels.

8 tablespoons olive oil
4 shallots, finely chopped
12 cherry tomatoes
500 g (1 lb) fresh wheat-free millet spaghetti
2 garlic cloves, crushed
500 g (1 lb) mixed mushrooms (oyster, horse mushrooms, shiitake, chanterelle), thickly sliced
2 tablespoons chopped parsley
handful of basil leaves
sea salt and freshly ground black pepper
extra virgin olive oil, to serve

1 Heat the oil in a large frying-pan, add the shallots, and cook in the oil for 2–3 minutes or until just soft.

2 Meanwhile, preheat the grill. Put the cherry tomatoes on a baking sheet and cook under the grill until soft and just beginning to char.

3 Bring a pan of water to the boil, add the spaghetti and return to the boil for 3 minutes, or as specified on the packet instructions.

4 Add the garlic to the cooked shallots and cook for 1 further minute. Add the mushrooms and sauté quickly over a high heat for 2–3 minutes or until just soft. Add salt and pepper to taste and the chopped parsley, and toss together.

5 Drain the spaghetti the minute it is cooked and return to the pan. Add the mushrooms and tomatoes together with the basil leaves and toss together.

6 Serve the spaghetti in bowls, with a little extra virgin olive oil drizzled over. Eat immediately.

Serves 4
Preparation time: 10 minutes
Cooking time: 10 minutes

Guacamole Soft Tortilla Wraps

A rustic and thick guacamole is an ideal filler for Mexican-inspired wraps. Add ingredients such as chargrilled chicken or turkey, extra vegetables, refried beans, salad leaves and feta or mozzarella. For those who cannot tolerate wheat, use corn tacos instead of flour tortillas.

8 flour tortillas
3 large avocados
1 garlic clove, crushed
25 g (1 oz) sun dried tomatoes
25 g (1 oz) watercress, roughly chopped
1 small red onion, finely chopped
2 tablespoons lemon or lime juice
3 tablespoons low-fat bio yogurt
handful of lettuce leaves
2–3 tomatoes, halved and thickly sliced
sea salt and freshly ground black pepper

1 Preheat the oven to 180°C (350°F), Gas Mark 4. Wrap the tortillas in foil and warm in the oven for 15 minutes.

2 To make the guacamole, halve, stone and peel the avocados and roughly chop the flesh. Add the garlic, sun-dried tomatoes, watercress and red onion and mix together. Add the lemon juice, salt, pepper and yogurt and mix together to form a rough purée.

3 Cover each warm tortilla with lettuce leaves, a large spoonful of guacamole and sliced tomatoes and firmly roll up and serve, or wrap in greaseproof paper and take away to eat on the move.

Serves 4
Preparation time: 15 minutes
Cooking time: 15 minutes

Mango and Avocado Salad with Smoked Chicken

2 ripe avocados
2 tablespoons lemon juice
1 small mango
3 tablespoons olive oil
1 teaspoon wholegrain mustard
1 teaspoon clear honey
2 teaspoons cider vinegar
handful of watercress
50 g (2 oz) cooked beetroot, finely sliced
175 g (6 oz) smoked chicken, thinly sliced
sea salt and freshly ground black pepper

1 Halve, stone and peel the avocados. Either slice or dice the avocado flesh and place in a shallow bowl with the lemon juice.

2 Cut the mango in half either side of the central stone, peel away the skin and slice or dice the flesh.

3 Mix the olive oil with the wholegrain mustard, honey, vinegar, salt and pepper and mix well. Remove the avocado from the lemon juice and mix the juice into the dressing.

4 Arrange the watercress and beetroot on 4 plates or in a salad bowl and add the avocado and mango flesh. Drizzle the vinaigrette over the salad and top with the slices of smoked chicken. Serve immediately.

Serves 4
Preparation time: 15 minutes

Spinach and Goat's Cheese with Wholewheat Pasta

1 Blanch the spinach leaves in boiling water for 1 minute. Drain the leaves, squeezing out any excess water and roughly chop. Mix the spinach with the grated nutmeg, goat's cheese, crème fraîche and mustard.

2 Bring a pan of water to the boil, add the pasta, return to the boil and cook for 4–5 minutes until tender, or as specified on the packet instructions. Drain well.

3 Return the hot pasta immediately to the pan and add the spinach mixture, salt, pepper and pine kernels and toss together. Add the parsley and Parmesan and a touch more grated nutmeg and serve while still piping hot.

Serves 4
Preparation time: 10 minutes
Cooking time: 8 minutes

500 g (1 lb) baby spinach leaves
pinch of grated nutmeg
125 g (4 oz) goat's cheese, roughly chopped
150 ml (¼ pint) low-fat crème fraîche
2 teaspoons Dijon mustard
500 g (1 lb) fresh wholewheat pasta
75 g (3 oz) pine kernels, toasted
1 tablespoon chopped parsley
2 tablespoons grated Parmesan cheese
sea salt and freshly ground black pepper

Wilted Spring Greens with Ginger, Sesame and Brown Rice

Green, red and white cabbage are all vital vegetables to include in everyday eating. Spring greens are more delicate and cook quickly, but in their absence use savoy or white cabbage.

250 g (8 oz) brown rice
10 cm (4 in) piece of kombu seaweed
1 onion, finely chopped
3 tablespoons olive oil
2 garlic cloves, crushed
325 g (11 oz) spring greens, shredded
7.5 cm (3 in) piece fresh root ginger, finely chopped
4 tablespoons tamari or soy sauce
1 tablespoon sesame oil
2 tablespoons sesame seeds, toasted
freshly ground black pepper

1 Put the brown rice in a large pan of boiling water with the kombu and bring to the boil. Reduce the heat a little and cook at a fast simmer for 30 minutes. When the rice is just cooked and still retains a bite, drain well (reserving some of the cooking water) and discard the seaweed.

2 In a large pan or wok, gently cook the onion in the oil until golden brown and crisp. Add the garlic and continue to cook gently for 1 minute, stirring constantly, to flavour the oil. Do not allow the garlic to burn.

3 Add the spring greens and ginger and stir-fry for 1–2 minutes or until the greens are just wilted.

4 Combine the tamari or soy sauce, sesame oil and 6 tablespoons of reserved cooking water; add to the vegetables and stir-fry for 1 further minute.

5 Remove from the heat and toss the cooked rice and the wilted spring greens together. Spoon into serving bowls and top with toasted sesame seeds and black pepper. Serve immediately or chill and serve cold.

Serves 4
Preparation time: 15 minutes
Cooking time: 30 minutes

Papaya Soya Smoothie

Papaya is the ideal fruit to start the day. It has excellent digestive properties and is rich in vitamins A and C, plus potassium. Either eat it simply cut in half with a squeeze of lime on top, the seeds scooped out and discarded, or try making a quick smoothie, which can be drunk while you get ready for the day ahead.

1 papaya
2 bananas, peeled and chopped
300 ml (½ pint) low-fat bio yogurt
300 ml (½ pint) soya milk or apple juice
ice cubes, to serve

1 Halve the papaya, scoop out the seeds and discard. Using a spoon, scoop out the flesh and add to a blender or food processor.

2 Add the chopped bananas to the blender with the yogurt. Blend the mixture for 1 minute until smooth and frothy.

3 Add the soya milk or apple juice to the blender or food processor and blend together once more.

4 Pour the papaya smoothie into tall tumblers containing ice cubes and serve immediately.

Serves 4
Preparation time: 5 minutes

Poached Guava with Yogurt Brûlée

Guavas are highly perfumed and delicious fruits. Most people are used to the pink-fleshed varieties found in cans; however, buy them fresh and they are green skinned and most often have cream-coloured flesh. Poach them gently until soft and serve with yogurt. Of course, you can always use the canned ones, but they are heavily loaded with sugar syrup.

375 g (12 oz) Greek yogurt or fromage frais
4–6 tablespoons dark muscovado or molasses
    sugar
3 small fresh ripe guavas, thinly peeled and
    halved
1 tablespoon unrefined raw cane caster sugar
150 ml (¼ pint) apple juice

1 Spoon the yogurt or fromage frais into one shallow heatproof dish or 6 individual dishes and smooth the top. Sprinkle the brown muscovado or molasses sugar over the top and refrigerate overnight or until required.

2 Place the guava halves in a saucepan with the caster sugar and apple juice. Cover the pan and poach the fruit gently for 12–15 minutes, turning the guavas once, until soft and tender when prodded with a sharp knife.

3 Remove the fruit from the heat, quarter the guavas and spread over a baking sheet.

4 Preheat the grill. When hot, place the dishes of yogurt on the baking sheet with the guavas and grill close to the heat for 1–2 minutes or until the sugar on the brûlées has melted and is bubbling in places and the guavas have begun to brown. Either serve the yogurt brûlée immediately with the poached guavas, or chill both overnight and serve cold.

Serves 6
Preparation time: 10 minutes
Cooking time: 18 minutes

beat the blues

Melancholy, gloom or despair... whatever you call it, at some time or another almost everyone feels a bit down. The links between depression and diet are twofold. On the one hand, some foods may cause depression; on the other hand, when we feel low we tend to crave foods that will make things even worse. Food allergies, nutritional deficiencies and biochemical imbalances may all cause symptoms of depression.

In the United Kingdom one in six people suffer depression of some kind in the course of their lifetime and one in 20 experience clinical depression. Even more worryingly, it has been reported that 2 per cent of children under 12 experience depression and that as many as 5 per cent of teenagers also suffer from this debilitating disorder.

Depression is often the result of an unpleasant or traumatic event. The list of these common causes is endless, and individuals' reactions to these events are equally varied in intensity and duration. This condition is referred to as 'reactive' depression and is often a natural response to some external stress or tension. However, it becomes a matter of greater concern when recovery from an unpleasant experience lingers on and the depression continues for months or years instead of days or weeks.

Signs and symptoms of depression vary from person to person and can range from fatigue to insomnia, from feelings of worthlessness to irritability and anger. Often, depression is associated with physical aches and pains, as well as digestive problems, including diarrhoea, constipation and indigestion. In many cases there is no apparent external cause of depression. However, there may be other triggers.

Depression can take many forms and it is the various expressions that may give us clues as to the underlying cause, which may in turn point to a nutritional solution.

No get-up-and-go?

Apathy and lack of motivation are signs that suggest the brain's depression may be due to long-term stress. Stress can deplete the body's supplies of the adrenal gland hormones, adrenaline (epinephrine) and noradrenaline (norepinephrine), and low levels of these hormones are associated with depression. This is where the amino acid tyrosine comes in. Tyrosine is found in foods including wheatgerm, ricotta and cottage cheese, yogurt and milk.

Tyrosine is one of the amino acids that can cross the blood-brain barrier. This barrier is the body's special protective mechanism for preventing any undesirable chemicals from reaching precious brain tissue.

Once in the brain, tyrosine is transformed into noradrenaline, and it is this essential stress-busting chemical that can improve moods and lift depression.

It is important to note that tyrosine-rich foods need vitamin B3, vitamin C, copper and most importantly folic acid for the tyrosine to be converted to mood-enhancing noradrenaline. Interestingly, nature provides good supplies of these co-factors in tyrosine-rich foods, such as milk, yogurt, cheeses and wheat. Nevertheless, it is a good idea to have plenty of other folic acid-rich foods as well in the diet just to make sure. Brewers' yeast and green leafy vegetables are especially good sources of folic acid.

So, if depression is characterized by lack of drive, apathy and no get-up-and-go, then a diet rich in tyrosine foods, together with the sources of the co-factor vitamins and minerals will supply the key nutrients needed for the brain to think more quickly and clearly.

Feeling down?

Anxiety, insomnia, sadness, gloom and despair are symptoms familiar to many sufferers of depression. This may be linked to insufficient levels of the neurotransmitter serotonin, which is known to lift depression, ease tension and encourage sleep.

Serotonin is produced from the amino acid tryptophan which we obtain from our food. Tryptophan is another amino acid that can cross the blood-brain barrier and this is encouraged by sweet foods and refined carbohydrates. This is why many people who are depressed crave sweets and eat lots of carbohydrates. It is far better, however, to eat tryptophan-rich foods such as eggs, cottage cheese, oats and turkey.

As with tyrosine, tryptophan-rich foods need other nutrients in order to produce the mood-lifting serotonin. Vitamin B6, folic acid and magnesium as well as complex carbohydrates are the key nutrients here. So it is necessary to complement tryptophan-rich foods with brown rice, rye bread and wholemeal pasta to get the full effect of the nutrients in them. Add to this wheatgerm and bananas to supply the most important co-factor, vitamin B6.

It is interesting to note that many modern antidepressant drugs, including Prozac, work on the principle of keeping serotonin circulating in the brain in order to relieve depression. Foods which contain tryptophan, on the other hand, actually encourage the production of serotonin and therefore have a similar effect to these drugs.

Food allergies

There is now a large body of scientific evidence suggesting that food sensitivities may contribute to depression. These should be investigated, particularly if the depression is accompanied by an inability to think clearly, poor concentration, lack of energy and lethargy. As food allergies can irritate the digestive tract, the sufferer may also have diarrhoea, constipation, bloating or indigestion. In children, frequent ear, nose and throat infections, and dark circles under the eyes are key signs to look for. A constant runny nose is another pointer to a food sensitivity.

Gluten, a protein found in wheat, rye, oats and barley, together with dairy products such as milk, cheese, yogurt, butter and milk chocolate, appear to be the two main culprits of food-related depression. Even though milk and cheese are important sources of the key antidepression amino acids tyrosine and tryptophan, for some people these foods may actually be causing their depression.

To test for food sensitivities follow the instructions on page 31. If symptoms are alleviated by giving up a particular food and return when the food is reintroduced, try taking a complete break from the food for a couple of months and then reintroduce and check your body's response. (See page 32 for alternatives to gluten and dairy products.)

Sugar slump

When depressed, many people use sweets to cheer themselves up, but this may actually be making their depression worse. Sugar is needed by the brain for fuel, but the brain wants the sugar delivered at a constant and even pace. Sweets, chocolates and desserts cause the amount of sugar arriving in the brain to be too high. When the body attempts to regulate the sugar flow, it often overcompensates, leaving too little sugar to feed the brain. When this happens many people feel down, and often reach for the chocolates to repeat the whole cycle.

Tips

If you suffer from depression:

Eat foods rich in tyrosine and tryptophan. Eat complex carbohydrates and eat oily fish 2–3 times a week. Research suggests that some depressed people are lacking in omega-3 essential fatty acids.

Exercise to increase circulation to the brain. Walking, swimming or similar activities lift depression.

Keep the mind active. Take part in social events, join an evening class, visit friends or family.

Get plenty of rest.

Avoid foods rich in saturated fats, which interfere with blood flow to the brain.

Cut out sugar, sweets, alcohol, also caffeine, which lowers tyrosine levels in the body and raises stress.

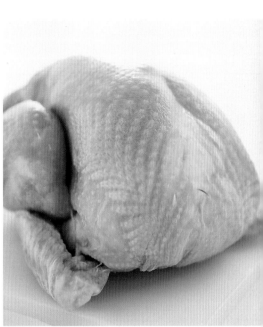

Foods in focus

Protein foods that contain the amino acids tryptophan and tyrosine are the key focus in this chapter for combating depression.

Dairy products

Milk and milk products are excellent sources of calcium, phosphorus, complete protein (contains all the essential amino acids), and lots of B vitamins.

Milk is an extremely good source of tyrosine, the amino acid that converts in the brain to noradrenaline (norepinephrine). It has the effect of increasing mental alertness, stimulating the brain to think more quickly and clearly, and increasing motivation. There is the same amount of this brain-boosting amino acid in all kinds of milk, but for the body to absorb calcium a small amount of fat is required, so semi-skimmed milk is the best choice.

As well as the motivating amino acid tyrosine, yogurt contains the B complex vitamins, plus more

A and D than milk. A small pot of yogurt contains 20 per cent of the RDA of calcium, which acts as a natural tranquillizer and helps with insomnia. Flavoured yogurts tend to be sweetened with lots of sugar and are best avoided.

Cheese is made by separating most of the curd, or milk solids, from the whey or water part of the milk. Most cheeses contain between two and three times more tyrosine and tryptophan than milk, so you need to eat less for mood-lifting effects. The low-fat varieties are preferable as they can increase mental energy without clogging the arteries that feed the brain.

Turkey

Chicken and turkey meat are both high in good-quality protein and lower in fat than beef and pork. In addition, turkey meat is one of the richest sources of the amino acid tryptophan and consequently is important for producing the neurotransmitter

serotonin that relieves depression. Turkey is also rich in the minerals phosphorus, iron, copper, zinc and magnesium, all of which are important for healthy nerves.

Remember that although poultry is a good, low-fat source of protein, turkey and chicken skin is almost one-third saturated fat. Saturated fats can clog arteries and make delivering nutrients to the brain difficult. Removing the skin reduces the amount of fat. When possible, buy organic poultry to avoid any added chemicals that may interfere with brain function (see page 25).

Oats

Oats contain high levels of both mood-lifting tryptophan and carbohydrates, which encourage the absorption of tryptophan into the brain. They also contain some B vitamins, calcium, magnesium and potassium, all of which are vital for healthy nerves. Because oats are digested slowly they help to maintain an even supply of energy to the brain by sustaining blood sugar levels.

Oats also contain antioxidants. These fight free radicals in the human body and account for the fact that oatmeal is very stable and its quality can be maintained when stored well in a closed container.

Wheatgerm

Wheatgerm is the nutritious kernel at the heart of the wheat grain, which sprouts when planted. Flour millers remove the germ as well as the bran, the outer coat of the wheat kernel, during refining. Wheatgerm is rich in the amino acids tyrosine and tryptophan, plus the vitamins and minerals needed to make the neurotransmitters noradrenaline (norepinephrine) and serotonin. One hundred grams (3½ oz) of wheatgerm supplies 90 per cent of the (RDA) for magnesium, 165 per cent of RDAs for B6 and folic acid. All three of these nutrients are needed to convert tryptophan to serotonin. Wheatgerm also contains 113 per cent of the RDA for zinc, known to alleviate depression.

Eggs

Eggs are an excellent source of complete protein, since they contain the right proportions of all the essential amino acids used by the brain to build neurotransmitters. In particular, eggs are a good source of tryptophan, which is needed to make the neurotransmitter serotonin – the antidepressant, mood stabilizer and sleep enhancer. Eggs also contain the antioxidant vitamins A and E, which can protect precious brain cells against the effects of free radicals.

Eggs fell from favour a few years ago when scientists assumed that eating foods high in cholesterol would raise cholesterol levels in the body. Recent research suggests that eating foods high in saturated fat (meats and high-fat cheeses) have a much greater impact on raising cholesterol levels than eating high-cholesterol foods like eggs. Although eggs do contain some saturated fat, gram per gram it is much less than meat. It has also been found that free-range eggs, produced by chickens exposed to daylight, are lower in cholesterol than eggs from intensively reared chickens.

For maximum benefit eggs should be boiled or poached but definitely not fried; frying creates free radicals and destroys many of the nutrients.

menu to beat the blues

Breakfast
porridge oats (oatmeal) made with
 semi-skimmed or soya milk

Lunch
Vegetable Frittata-stuffed Focaccia
 (*see page 52*)
mixed salad

Dinner
Red Pesto Turkey and Chickpea Mash
 (*see page 115*)
or Grilled Vegetables with Goat's
 Cheese (*see page 111*)
Brown Rice Pudding with Sultanas
 and Almonds (*see page 116*)

Snacks
Smoked Mackerel and Cottage
 Cheese Pâté with Rye Bread
 (*see page 110*)

Smoked Mackerel and Cottage Cheese Pâté with Rye Bread

Cottage cheese is low in fat and is an ideal base for dips and smooth, spreadable pâtés. This pâté can be made in advance and kept in the refrigerator for 2–3 days.

375 g (12 oz) smoked mackerel
2 celery sticks, finely chopped
200 g (7 oz) cottage cheese
1 tablespoon capers
25 g (1 oz) gherkins, finely chopped
½ teaspoon freshly ground black pepper, or to taste
1 tablespoon chopped chives

1 Remove any bones from the mackerel, discard the skin and flake the fish. Put the fish in a blender with the celery and blend together to a rough purée.

2 Add the cottage cheese and capers and blend together to a rough pâté.

3 Remove the mackerel pâté from the blender and stir in the gherkins, black pepper and chives.

4 Spoon the pâté into small individual dishes or a large serving dish and chill for 1–2 hours before serving. Serve with rye bread, radishes and cornichons.

Serves 4–6
Preparation time: 10 minutes

Grilled Vegetables with Goat's Cheese

Goat's cheese is far easier to digest than cow's milk cheese. It melts to a molten, oozing nugget of cheese that goes well with roasted vegetables or plain salads.

3 courgettes, thickly sliced
2 red peppers, deseeded and thickly sliced
1 fennel bulb, finely sliced
2 tablespoons olive oil
4 plum tomatoes, quartered
25 g (1 oz) peas
175 g (6 oz) goat's, halloumi or feta cheese
5 tablespoons extra virgin olive oil
1 tablespoon lemon juice
2 tablespoons balsamic vinegar
1 tablespoon chopped mint
sea salt and freshly ground black pepper
mint sprig, to garnish

1 Toss the courgettes, red pepper and fennel together. Drizzle with olive oil and spread in a roasting tin. Grill the vegetables for 6–8 minutes, turning from time to time until they are brown in places but not too soft. Add the tomatoes and continue to grill for 5 minutes until all the vegetables are well browned.

2 Blanch the peas in boiling water for 2 minutes, then drain well and add to the grilled vegetables. Season with salt and pepper and toss together. Put the vegetables in an ovenproof dish or individual dishes.

3 Thickly slice the cheese and lay the slices on top of the vegetables. Place under a hot grill and grill for 1–2 minutes until just bubbling.

4 Mix the extra virgin olive oil, lemon juice and balsamic vinegar together. Season to taste with salt and pepper and drizzle over the vegetables. Sprinkle the mint over the cheese and vegetables and serve while still warm, garnished with a sprig of mint.

Serves 4
Preparation time: 15 minutes
Cooking time: 15–17 minutes

Millet Patties with Sheep's Cheese

250 g (8 oz) millet
1 onion, finely chopped
1 tablespoon olive oil
1 garlic clove, crushed
1 teaspoon dried mixed herbs
1 litre (1¾ pints) vegetable stock or water
3 eggs
2 tablespoons chopped parsley
125 g (4 oz) sheep's cheese (eg manchego) or any
    hard cheese, cut into 12 pieces
125 g (4 oz) fine wholemeal breadcrumbs
vegetable oil, for shallow frying
1 quantity Tomato and Red Pepper Sauce
    (*see page 51*)
handful of basil or flat parsley leaves
sea salt and freshly ground black pepper
1–2 tablespoons grated sheep's cheese, to serve

1 Dry-fry the millet grains in a hot pan for 1–2 minutes, shaking the pan frequently. Remove from the pan and set aside.

2 Gently fry the onion in the oil until golden brown. Add the garlic and millet and coat in the oil. Add the herbs and stock and bring to the boil. Boil for 5 minutes, then reduce the heat, cover and simmer for 30–35 minutes or until the millet is soft and tender and the liquid has been absorbed. Leave to cool.

3 When the millet is cold, beat two of the eggs into the millet with the parsley, salt and pepper. Tightly form some millet mixture around each piece of sheep's cheese to form 12 patties. Beat the remaining egg and roll the patties in the egg and then in the breadcrumbs to coat them completely. Refrigerate for 1–2 hours.

4 Heat the oil for frying in a large pan and cook 4–6 patties at a time until golden brown on the outside. Remove from the oil and drain on kitchen paper. Serve the hot patties topped with the piping hot tomato and red pepper sauce and basil leaves.

Serves 4
Preparation time: 30 minutes, plus chilling
Cooking time: about 1 hour

Roasted Vegetables with Ricotta

Ricotta is a creamy mild cheese that teams well with vegetables and can also be used in desserts.

1 large aubergine, roughly chopped
2 red onions, cut into thick wedges
2 red peppers, deseeded and roughly chopped
1 yellow pepper, deseeded and roughly chopped
2 courgettes, thickly sliced
2 tablespoons olive oil
175 g (6 oz) bulgar wheat
1 garlic clove, halved
10 cherry tomatoes
1 tablespoon chopped basil
2 tablespoons chopped parsley
125 g (4 oz) ricotta cheese
sea salt and freshly ground black pepper
extra virgin olive oil, to serve

1 Preheat the oven to 220°C (425°F), Gas Mark 7. Put all the prepared vegetables into a large roasting tin and toss together. Drizzle the olive oil over the vegetables, season with salt and pepper, and roast in the preheated oven for 20 minutes, stirring occasionally.

2 Meanwhile put the bulgar wheat in a pan of water with the halved garlic clove and gently bring to the boil. Reduce the heat and simmer for 4–5 minutes. Remove from the heat and drain well, discarding the garlic.

3 Add the cherry tomatoes to the roasting vegetables and cook for a further 8–10 minutes or until all the vegetables are well roasted.

4 Put the drained bulgar wheat in a bowl and season well with salt and pepper. Add the basil and parsley and mix together.

5 Spoon the bulgar wheat on to serving plates and top with roasted vegetables. While the vegetables are still hot, top with a spoonful of ricotta. Season with black pepper, drizzle extra virgin olive oil over the ricotta and serve immediately.

Serves 4
Preparation time: 15 minutes
Cooking time: 30 minutes

Eggs Florentine with Cheese Sauce

Eggs are highly nutritious. The yolks are high in vitamins A, D and E and some vitamin B. An alternative, dairy-free sauce for the spinach is Tomato and Red Pepper Sauce (*see page 51*).

875 g (1¾ lb) young spinach, rinsed and drained
¼ teaspoon grated nutmeg
4 large eggs
300 ml (½ pint) milk
25 g (1 oz) plain or gluten-free flour
25 g (1 oz) butter
50 g (2 oz) Parmesan or Cheddar cheese, grated
2 tablespoons dry wholemeal breadcrumbs
sea salt and freshly ground black pepper

1 Preheat the oven to 190°C (375°F), Gas Mark 5. Lightly grease a 1 litre (1¾ pint) ovenproof dish or 4 individual dishes.

2 Heat the spinach gently in a covered pan until just wilted. Place in a sieve and press out as much liquid as possible. Roughly chop the spinach, season with salt, pepper and grated nutmeg and spoon it into the bottom of the ovenproof dish or dishes. Make four indentations in the spinach and break an egg into each.

3 Put the milk, flour and butter in a pan and bring to a slow boil, whisking continually. Keep whisking as the sauce begins to boil, and continue cooking for a further 2–3 minutes or until the sauce has thickened. Remove the pan from the heat and season with salt and pepper. Stir in three-quarters of the cheese.

4 Pour the sauce over the eggs. Sprinkle with the remaining cheese and the breadcrumbs. Cook in the preheated oven for 15 minutes or until the sauce is bubbling and the eggs are cooked.

Serves 4
Preparation time: 15 minutes
Cooking time: 30 minutes

Red Pesto Turkey and Chickpea Mash

1 Bring the chickpeas to the boil in a large pan of boiling water. Boil fast for 15 minutes, then reduce the heat, cover and simmer for 1½–2 hours or until cooked and soft. Add extra water during cooking if necessary. Drain well.

2 Fry the onion in olive oil until golden brown. Add 1 crushed garlic clove and cook for 1 minute before adding the cumin seeds and drained chickpeas. Roughly mash the ingredients together. Add the yogurt, coriander, salt and pepper and mix together. Keep warm.

3 Meanwhile, place the turkey in a wide, shallow saucepan with the bay leaves and lemon. Cover with cold water and slowly bring to a fast simmer. Remove from the heat and let stand for 10 minutes. Check the turkey is cooked through.

4 Put the remaining crushed garlic in a blender with the sun-dried tomatoes and basil and blend to a rough purée. Add the pine kernels, Parmesan and pepper and blend briefly before adding the extra virgin olive oil and blending once more.

5 Remove the turkey from the poaching liquid and serve sliced on top of the chickpea mash with the red pesto drizzled over. Garnish with flat leaf parsley.

Serves 4
Preparation time: 20 minutes
Cooking time: 1¾–2¼ hours

150 g (6 oz) dried chickpeas, soaked overnight, rinsed and drained
1 small onion, finely chopped
2 tablespoons olive oil
2 garlic cloves, crushed
1 teaspoon cumin seeds
3 tablespoons yogurt or low-fat crème fraîche
2 tablespoons chopped fresh coriander
4 x 150 g (5 oz) turkey fillets
2 bay leaves
1 small lemon, halved
50 g (2 oz) sun-dried tomatoes or red peppers in oil, drained and chopped
15 g (½ oz) basil leaves
1 tablespoon pine kernels
1 tablespoon grated Parmesan cheese
4 tablespoons extra virgin olive oil
sea salt and freshly ground black pepper
flat leaf parsley, to garnish

Brown Rice Pudding with Sultanas and Almonds

1 Preheat the oven to 180°C (350°F) Gas Mark 4. Lightly butter a 1.2 litre (2 pint) ovenproof dish.

2 Rinse the rice well and put it in a pan of water. Bring to the boil, cook for 15 minutes, then drain well. Return the rice to the pan with the milk and sugar and bring slowly to the boil.

3 Remove from the heat and pour into the prepared ovenproof dish. Add the sultanas and stir together. Sprinkle the nutmeg over the milk and dot the top with pieces of butter, if using.

4 Cook in the centre of the preheated oven for 1½–2 hours, stirring twice. Once the rice is soft and tender, remove it from the oven and sprinkle the flaked almonds and stem ginger over the top of the pudding.

5 When serving the pudding, stir the almonds and ginger into the rice. Serve with low-fat crème fraîche or fromage frais.

Serves 4–6
Preparation time: 10 minutes
Cooking time: 2–2½ hours

Milk puddings are a childhood favourite but they can be updated to create a more sophisticated dish. This recipe uses brown rice instead of the more usual pudding rice. It naturally takes longer to cook and benefits from initially boiling the rice and then adding it to the milk. Serve with mixed berries or poached fruit. If liked, cook the pudding without sugar and sweeten to taste with honey when serving.

75 g (3 oz) brown rice
900 ml (1½ pints) organic milk
25 g (1 oz) soft light brown sugar
75 g (3 oz) sultanas
½ teaspoon grated nutmeg
15 g (½ oz) butter (optional)
3 tablespoons flaked almonds, toasted
50 g (2 oz) stem ginger, finely chopped

Wheatgerm, Pineapple and Banana Booster

Like molasses and brewers' yeast, try to eat some wheatgerm every day. An easy way is to start the morning with a smoothie or muesli to which a little wheatgerm has been added.

2 tablespoons wheatgerm
1 tablespoon sesame seeds
2 bananas, peeled and roughly sliced
75 g (3 oz) pineapple pieces
450 ml (¾ pint) apple juice
300 ml (½ pint) yogurt

1 Preheat the grill. Spread the wheatgerm and sesame seeds over a baking sheet and gently toast, stirring a couple of times until the sesame seeds have begun to turn a golden brown colour. Remove from the grill and leave to cool.

2 Put the bananas in a blender with the pieces of pineapple and blend together to a rough purée.

3 Add the apple juice and blend once more until you have a smoothish juice. Add the yogurt and the cooled wheatgerm and sesame seeds, blend once again and pour into tall glasses to serve.

Serves 4
Preparation time: 10 minutes
Cooking time: 5 minutes

Milk Junket with Rhubarb

Junket is a very old English pudding. It can be flavoured with coffee, chocolate or fruit purées, but vanilla is undoubtedly the best variation. Opt for vegetarian rennet (available in health food stores) and use skimmed, goat's or soya milk if preferred. Serve with any poached fresh or dried fruit.

600 ml (1 pint) organic milk
1 vanilla pod
3 tablespoons unrefined raw cane sugar or
    clear honey
10 drops vegetarian rennet
750 g (1½ lb) rhubarb, roughly chopped
juice and finely grated rind of 1 unwaxed orange
1 tablespoon flaked almonds, toasted

1 Put the milk and vanilla pod in a saucepan and heat slowly until just warm, but not boiling. Add 1 tablespoon of the sugar or honey to the pan and stir gently to dissolve.

2 Remove the pan from the heat and remove the vanilla pod. Split it in half lengthways, scrape out the vanilla seeds and add to the milk. Mix well to distribute the seeds.

3 Add the rennet to the vanilla milk and stir well. Pour the mixture into a serving bowl or into small individual bowls or moulds, allow to cool and then put in the refrigerator until set.

4 Put the rhubarb in a saucepan with the orange juice and the grated orange rind. Add the remaining sugar or honey and gently heat for 6–8 minutes, or until the juice begins to bubble and the pieces of rhubarb have begun to soften and are cooked to the centre but still retain their shape.

5 Immediately remove from the heat and leave to cool. When the rhubarb is cool, serve with a large spoonful of junket and topped with toasted almonds.

Serves 4–6
Preparation time: 20 minutes, plus chilling
Cooking time: 20 minutes

Apricot Fool with Ground Linseeds

Yogurt makes quick and simple puddings that are good for you, too. Use live bio yogurt for the best immune system and digestive properties. It is rich in minerals and fat-soluble vitamins. This recipe uses dried apricots, but opt for fresh apricots when in season; stone them, simmer them gently in 2 tablespoons of apple juice and use as described here.

175 g (6 oz) dried apricots
200 ml (7 fl oz) apple juice or water
finely grated rind of ½ lemon
450 ml (¾ pint) thick yogurt
2 teaspoons linseeds
oat biscuits, to serve

1 Put the apricots in a saucepan with the apple juice or water and simmer slowly for 10–12 minutes, or until the apricots are soft but not overcooked. Add extra apple juice or water if necessary. Roughly mash or blend the apricots to a purée. Set aside to cool.

2 Add the lemon rind to the yogurt and mix together until well combined. Grind the linseeds using a pestle and mortar until crushed and split but not a powder. If you don't have a pestle and mortar, put the linseeds in a small bowl and crush them with the end of a rolling-pin.

3 Add the cooled apricots to the yogurt mixture and roughly fold into the yogurt to obtain a marbled effect. Add three-quarters of the linseeds halfway through folding in, then spoon the fool into 4 dessert glasses and chill for 2 hours. Serve topped with the remaining linseeds and oat biscuits.

Serves 4
Preparation time: 15 minutes
Cooking time: 10–12 minutes

Blackberry and Oat Layer

A quicker version of this recipe uses 2 tablespoons homemade muesli in place of the roasted oats. If cinnamon or nutmeg is a favourite spice, add to the cooling oats. You could replace the blackberries with any seasonal berries or thawed frozen fruit.

25 g (1 oz) oats
3 tablespoons clear honey
15 g (½ oz) stem ginger, roughly chopped
175 g (6 oz) blackberries
150 ml (¼ pint) thick yogurt
150 ml (¼ pint) low-fat crème fraîche
grated rind of ½ lemon

1 Preheat the oven to 180°C (350°F), Gas Mark 4. Mix the oats with 2 tablespoons of the honey and spread over a baking sheet. Cook in the preheated oven for 10–15 minutes, stirring once or twice.

2 Remove from the oven, add the ginger to the oats and leave to cool. Roughly crush the blackberries. Stir the oats to break up any large lumps.

3 Mix the yogurt and crème fraîche with the grated lemon rind until well combined and sweeten to taste with the remaining honey.

4 Layer the mashed blackberries and cooled oats with the yogurt mixture in a serving bowl or individual dessert glasses. Refrigerate for 1–2 hours.

Serves 4
Preparation time: 20 minutes, plus chilling
Cooking time: 15 minutes

Blueberry Compote with Sweet Porridge and Nuts

1 Put the blueberries in a pan with 2 tablespoons of the caster sugar or honey and heat very gently for 6–8 minutes or until the juice from the berries begins to run. Remove from the heat and leave to stand while you make the porridge.

2 Put the oats in a pan with the milk or water, add sugar to taste and bring to the boil, stirring constantly. Simmer gently for 6–8 minutes, stirring occasionally, and add extra milk or water if liked.

3 Serve the porridge topped with the blueberries, the toasted nuts, a little soft dark brown sugar and the wheatgerm, if using. Pour some milk, buttermilk or yogurt over the porridge and serve.

Serves 4
Preparation time: 10 minutes
Cooking time: 15 minutes

This smooth, creamy porridge with fresh fruit and nuts can be served at any time of the day. For extra spice add a stick of cinnamon when cooking the porridge, and if liked add raisins to the oats at the beginning of cooking and serve with a squeeze of lemon juice.

125 g (4 oz) blueberries
2–3 tablespoons unrefined raw caster sugar or honey, to taste
150 g (5 oz) rolled oats
1 litre (1¾ pints) milk, water or half milk and half water
3 tablespoons roughly chopped hazelnuts or almonds, toasted
1–3 tablespoons soft dark brown sugar
1–2 tablespoons toasted wheatgerm (optional)
milk, buttermilk or thin bio yogurt, to serve

Glossary

absorption – The process by which the body assimilates nutrients via the digestive tract to the bloodstream for nourishing the cells of the body.

additive – A general term for chemicals (natural or artificial) used to preserve, colour, flavour or sweeten food products.

adrenaline – A hormone secreted by the adrenal glands resulting in a stress reaction. Typical effects include increased heart rate and blood pressure plus elevated blood sugar level. Also called epinephrine.

allergen – A substance that causes a sensitivity reaction.

allergy – An inappropriate physical or mental reaction to certain chemicals in food, drugs, dust, pollution and metals.

amino acids – The building blocks of proteins, used in the body to make neurotransmitters. Protein-rich foods include meat, poultry, milk, cheese and fish.

anthocyanidin – A flavonoid responsible for the purple colour in fruits and berries; a potent antioxidant.

anthoxanthin – A flavonoid found in potatoes, yellow-skinned onions, grapefruit and soya beans. It helps to enhance immunity and balance hormones in the body.

anti-nutrients – Foods or drinks that either prevent nutrients from being absorbed or use excessive amounts of a nutrient, thus making it unavailable for other mental and physical processes. Examples are alcohol and caffeine.

antioxidants – Nutrients, including vitamins A, C and E and the minerals selenium and zinc, that help to disarm free radicals, thus reducing the oxidative damage thought to be responsible for many of the degenerative diseases.

aspartame – An artificial sweetener found in soft drinks, sweets and confectionery.

B complex – The group of B vitamins, including vitamins B1, B2, B3, B5, B6 and B12 involved in energy production, needed to fuel brain power.

beta-carotene – A carotenoid pigment found in dark green and orange fruits and vegetables. In the body, beta-carotene is converted to vitamin A and is an important antioxidant.

biochemical – Refers to chemical and physiological processes that take place in the body.

blood-brain barrier – A barrier that selectively allows the passage of materials from the blood to the brain. Its purpose is to protect the brain from toxins.

blood sugar – The sugar (or glucose) present in the blood that provides energy to the brain, muscles and tissues of the body.

boron – A mineral involved in calcium and magnesium absorption. It is needed by neurotransmitters for efficient travel between nerve cells. Boron is found in many fruits and vegetables.

brain – A mass of nervous tissue, the centre of sensation, thought, intelligence and emotion.

caffeine – A chemical stimulant found in coffee, tea and cola drinks. Initially, caffeine can stimulate mental alertness; however, it may also cause anxiety, irritability and depression.

calcium – The most abundant mineral in the body. It is important for building and maintaining bones and teeth, and for the release of neurotransmitters and contractions of muscles. Calcium can have a calming effect and is found in dairy products, including milk and cheese, as well as nuts.

carbohydrate – A substance found primarily in fruits and vegetables, and is the major source of energy in the diet.

cholesterol – An important component of cell membranes, cholesterol facilitates the transportation and absorption of key fatty acids. In excess, it can be a potential health problem, clogging the main arteries that feed the heart and brain.

circulation – The flow of blood around the body, ensuring the delivery of vital nutrients to muscles and organs, as well as clearing away toxins for excretion.

collagen – An important component of connective tissues, including the veins and arteries that carry nutrients to the brain.

digestion – The process by which the body takes food and breaks it down into smaller components to be used by the body. Proteins are broken down into amino acids, carbohydrates into simple sugars, and fats into fatty acids.

enzymes – Specific proteins that act as catalysts in promoting a chemical reaction in the body.

epinephrine – See adrenaline.

essential fatty acids – Fats required by the body that cannot be manufactured by the body but must be consumed in the diet. There are two types of essential fatty acids: omega-3 and omega-6.

excretion – The process by which the body eliminates waste products and toxins.

fat – A substance found primarily in animal, fish and dairy products, nuts and seeds. Fat is used by the body to manufacture body tissues and hormone-like substances to help regulate body functions.

fight-flight reaction – Another name for the stress survival reaction that increases the heart rate and elevates blood sugar levels to produce more energy to prepare the body to face stress.

flavonoids – A group of phytochemicals found in plants that give rise to yellow, red and purple colours in flowers, fruits, leaves and stems. There are two main groups: the anthoxanthins and the anthocyanidins. They are thought to have various health-promoting functions when eaten.

folic acid – A vitamin involved in many body processes including cell division and in particular in the development of the nervous system of the foetus. Folic acid deficiency has been associated with depression.

free radical – An atom or group of atoms that is very chemically active because it has an unpaired electron. Electrons usually revolve around the centre of an atom in pairs. When there is an unpaired electron, the atom attacks atoms in cells 'looking for another electron'. This can result in damage to cells in the body and brain. Free radicals are formed in the presence of heat during cooking, exposure to radiation and pollution.

free-range – Meat or eggs raised under strict standards for animal health and welfare.

glucose – A simple sugar molecule and the primary source of energy for the brain.

gluten – A protein found in wheat, rye, oats and barley that causes an allergic reaction in some people.

hydrogenated fats – Fats that have been chemically altered to convert them from liquid to solid form. The process can destroy the nutritional value of the fat and results in the formation of altered fatty acid molecules.

iron – A mineral primarily involved in transporting oxygen via the blood to muscles, tissues and the brain. Iron is found in liver, lean meat, leafy green vegetables, whole grains and molasses.

IQ – Intelligence quotient, a standardized measure of intelligence.

legume – A family of plants with seeds (peas or beans) in a pod.

lycopene – Closely related to beta-carotene, lycopene gives rise to the red colouring in vegetables, particularly tomatoes, and is thought to have a significant antioxidant role.

magnesium – A mineral that plays a critical role in energy production within the cells of the body.

One of the highest magnesium concentrations is in the brain with its high energy demands. Magnesium is found in tofu, seeds, nuts, whole grains and green leafy vegetables.

manganese – An essential mineral involved in blood sugar control, energy production and increased antioxidant activity.

millet – A grain used like wheat, which can be bought and used in the form of pasta, flour, flakes or kernels.

minerals – Inorganic substances needed in tiny amounts in the diet to maintain bodily functions and preserve the vigour of the heart, brain, and muscle and nerve systems.

nerve cell – *See* neuron.

neuron – A nerve cell consisting of a central cell body, plus tentacle-like structures which carry messages either towards the central body or away towards another neuron.

neurotransmitter – A chemical released from a nerve cell carrying a message to another cell or another part of the body. Neurotransmitters can affect physical movements as well as mental functions and moods.

noradrenaline – *See* norepinephrine.

norepinephrine – A hormone secreted by the adrenal glands resulting in a stress reaction. Also called noradrenaline.

nutrients – Chemical components present in foods that furnish the body with heat and energy, provide material for the growth and repair of the body tissues, and assist in the regulation of body processes. Carbohydrates, fats, proteins, vitamins, minerals and water are all nutrients.

omega-3 fatty acid – An essential fatty acid found in plant seeds and in oily fish.

omega-6 fatty acid – An essential fatty acid found in the seeds of plants.

organic food – Foods grown under specific regulations prohibiting the use of genetically modified foods and ingredients, chemical fertilizers, pesticides or growth-promoting hormones.

pesticide – A substance used to destroy crop pests, especially insects.

phosphorus – An essential mineral found in every cell. It helps to balance calcium and is involved in the production of energy and the transference of nerve impulses. Phosphorus is found in most protein-rich foods including milk, meat, fish, poultry, eggs, garlic, legumes and whole grains.

phytochemicals – A general term used to describe nutrients from plants that are not carbohydrates, proteins, fats, vitamins or minerals. These substances have recently been recognized to act as powerful antioxidants, protecting the body from free-radical damage.

potassium – A mineral involved in the functions of the kidney, heart, muscles and nerves. Potassium is found in fruits and vegetables.

protein – A nutrient that supplies the building material for the body, including muscles, skin, hair, nails and internal organs such as the heart and brain. Protein is made up of amino acids and is classified as 'complete' or 'incomplete' depending on the amount and ratio of the essential amino acids. Animal products are rich sources of protein.

quinoa – A South American seed used as a grain. It can be bought as flour or in the form of a kernel.

saccharin – An artificial sweetener used to sweeten many processed foods and drinks.

saturated fat – Fat that is solid at room temperature such as butter and lard. These fats have been linked with many chronic diseases.

serotonin – A neurotransmitter found in the brain that regulates relaxation, sleep and concentration.

sodium – An essential mineral found in every cell in the body. Sodium has many important functions including transporting oxygen and aiding digestion. Sodium helps keep calcium in a solution form that is necessary for nerve strength. It is found in virtually all foods but animal sources have more sodium than plant forms. Sodium is also found in sodium chloride or table salt. People rarely suffer from sodium deficiency and the more common problem is too much sodium, which may aggravate high blood pressure.

stimulant – A food or drink that has a stimulating effect on the body. A common stimulant is caffeine found in coffee, tea and cola drinks.

sugar – A simple carbohydrate found in most fruits and vegetables. During digestion carbohydrates are broken down into sugars. Types of sugars include glucose or 'blood sugar', fructose found in fruits and lactose, which is milk sugar.

synergy – An interaction between two or more nutrients where their combined action is greater than the sum of their individual actions.

theobromine – A stimulant which is found in coffee.

theophylline – A stimulant which is found in coffee.

toxin – A poison that hampers the body's ability to function. Many chemicals are toxins.

tryptophan – An essential amino acid used by the brain to produce serotonin.

tyrosine – An essential amino acid that converts into the neurotransmitter norepinephrine, which regulates the mood.

whole grains – Grains that have not been refined or processed in a way that leads to a reduction in their nutritional content.

vitamin – A nutrient essential for life and health.

vitamin A – A vitamin needed for good vision, growth, reproduction and immune function. Vitamin A is found in liver, kidney and whole milk.

vitamin B1 – A vitamin needed for energy production and nerve cell function. Vitamin B1 is found in soya beans, brown rice and sunflower seeds. Vitamin B1 is also known as thiamin.

vitamin B2 – A vitamin needed for energy production. It also plays an antioxidant role and is found in offal as well as almonds, mushrooms and whole grains. Vitamin B2 is also called riboflavin.

vitamin B3 – A vitamin that is involved in energy production and carbohydrate utilization. It is involved in the regulation of blood sugar, antioxidant mechanisms and detoxification reactions. It is found in legumes, whole grains and avocados. Vitamin B3 is also called niacin.

vitamin B5 – A vitamin that acts as an immune stimulant. It also stimulates the production of adrenal chemicals important for healthy nerves. Vitamin B5 can improve the body's ability to withstand stressful conditions. It is found in offal, brewers' yeast, egg yolks and whole grains. Vitamin B5 is also called pantothenic acid.

vitamin B6 – An extremely important B vitamin involved in the formation of body proteins and structural compounds, chemical transmitters in the nervous system, red blood cells and hormone-like compounds. Good sources of vitamin B6 include whole grains, legumes, bananas, seeds and nuts. Vitamin B6 is also called pyridoxine.

vitamin B12 – A vitamin essential in many body processes including production of red blood cells and the insulation sheath that surrounds nerve cells and speeds the conduction of the signals along nerve cells. Vitamin B12 is found in significant amounts only in animal foods, including liver, kidney, eggs, fish, cheese and meat. Tempeh, a fermented soya bean product, is an excellent source of vitamin B12 for vegetarians and vegans. Vitamin B12 is also called cobalamin.

vitamin C – A vitamin critical to immune function, the manufacture of some nerve-transmitting substances and the absorption and utilization of other nutritional factors. Vitamin C is a very important antioxidant. High levels are found in broccoli, peppers, potatoes, papaya and guava.

vitamin E – A vitamin that plays a key antioxidant role fighting free radicals. It is found in vegetable oils, seeds, nuts and whole grains.

zinc – A key mineral involved in over 200 different body functions. It is necessary for growth, immune function, wound healing, sensory functions and mental health. Good sources of zinc are oysters, shellfish and red meats, plus pumpkin seeds, whole grains and legumes.

Index

Acknowledgements

Executive Editor
Nicola Hill

Editor
Charlotte Wilson

Design Manager
Tokiko Morishima

Designer
Peter Gerrish

Special Photography
William Reavell

Stylist
Clare Hunt

Home Economist
Oona van den Berg

Production Controller
Martin Croshaw

Picture Researcher
Jennifer Veall

Picture Acknowledgements in Source Order

Octopus Publishing Group Limited/Frank Adam 122 bottom right/Colin Bowling 87 bottom right/Colin Gotts 87 bottom left/David Loftus 125/Gary Latham back jacket top left, 13 top left, 24 bottom left/Ian Wallace 11 bottom right, 19 top right, 33 top left, 93 bottom left/James Merrell front cover top right, 90 top left/ Mark Winwood 37 bottom left/ Peter Myers 29 top left/ Philip Webb 5 top right, 67 bottom right/Simon Smith 13 bottom right, 71 top right, 89 top right, 89 bottom right/William Adams-Lingwood 109 top right/William Reavell front jacket bottom left, back jacket bottom right, 5 top centre, 5 centre right, 10 top left, 11 bottom left, 12, 16, 17, 19 top left, 20, 25 top right, 26 top left, 27 bottom left, 30 top right, 32 bottom left, 40 bottom right, 40 bottom left, 41 bottom left, 41 bottom right, 42 top left, 42 bottom right, 43 top right, 43 bottom right, 44 top right, 44 top left, 45 bottom left, 46, 49, 50, 53, 54, 57, 58, 61, 62, 69 top right, 69 top left, 70 bottom left, 70 top left, 71 bottom left, 72, 75, 76, 79, 80, 83, 88 bottom right, 89 centre right, 90 bottom right, 91 bottom left, 91 bottom right, 92 top right, 92 bottom left, 93 top left, 93 top right, 94, 97, 98, 101, 105 bottom right, 105 bottom left, 107 top left, 107 top right, 108 bottom left, 108 top left, 109 bottom left, 111, 112, 115, 116, 119, 120/Image Bank/Color Day 39 top right/David de Lossy front cover top left, 36 top right/White/Packert 104 top right/Photodisc 9 top left, 31 bottom left, 45 top right, 86 top right, 106 top left/Getty Images Stone/David Hanover 38 bottom left/David Stewart 66 top right/Laurence Monneret 68 top left